Declutter Now!

ENDORSEMENTS

"*Declutter Now!* is the right book at the right time. In today's society, where more is touted as better, it can be difficult to cut through all the excess and uncover what really matters, but *Declutter Now!* lends a much needed hand. Packed with helpful tips, encouragement, humor, and personal stories, the reader will have no trouble figuring out that less can truly be more; more of what matters and means the most. Declutter every area of your life and enjoy more time, energy, freedom, finances, and joy to serve God. With each chapter covering a different area of your life, there's something for everyone. Let *Declutter Now!* help you start living a decluttered life today."

—*Lindsey Holder, Former Celebrity Assistant,*
Style Blogger at lindseyholder.com

"*Declutter Now!* reminded me that even baby steps are steps in the right direction. I may not have the time or energy to clean out a whole room, but I can clean out one drawer or one shelf of a closet. And when done consistently, each baby step adds up to a whole lot of forward motion!"

—*Carrie Daws, author of*
Crossing Values *and* Ryan's Crossing

"This book is born out of the real-life lessons of people just like you. Far from yet another how-to book, this is a philosophy of life that will bring you new levels of freedom...it will help you live the life God intended."
—*Dr. Brett Carlson, Executive Pastor, Mountain Ridge Church*

"Sherry and Lindon have found a wonderful means of taking the elements of real life concerns and putting them into simple layman's terms for any individual to apply immediately to their given circumstances. The examples provided, and sharing of their own stories, lends to the reader the prospect to relate to the authors. More importantly this relatedness provides for a more driven focus to occur where there is an ability to come to the other side of circumstances and have a dependence on God to bring them through. This vulnerability helps each of us remember that the Lord holds us in His hands always and with our willingness to listen and be open to a taking a step of faith we can experience the many blessings that await for us!"
—*Rebecca A. Richey, MAEd, MC, NCC PhD (ABD)*

DECLUTTER NOW!

Uncovering the Hidden Joy and Freedom in Your Life

By
Lindon & Sherry Gareis

AMBASSADOR INTERNATIONAL
GREENVILLE, SOUTH CAROLINA & BELFAST, NORTHERN IRELAND

www.ambassador-international.com

DECLUTTER NOW!
Uncovering the Hidden Joy
and Freedom in Your Life

ISBN: 978-1-62020-103-9
eISBN: 978-1-62020-153-4

Cover design: Matthew Mulder
Typesetting: Matthew Mulder
Author photo: Vanessa Jayne Photography, Glendale, AZ
E-book conversion: Anna Riebe

AMBASSADOR INTERNATIONAL
Emerald House
427 Wade Hampton Blvd.
Greenville, SC 29609, USA
www.ambassador-international.com

AMBASSADOR BOOKS
The Mount
2 Woodstock Link
Belfast, BT6 8DD, Northern Ireland, UK
www.ambassador-international.com

The colophon is a trademark of Ambassador

Acknowledgements

WE WISH TO EXTEND OUR sincere appreciation to our pastor and for-mer small group leader, Dr. Brett Carlson. Without fear or trepidation (at least none we could detect!), he turned his small group over to our tutelage so we could teach curriculum from what was still an unfinished book. Talk about a man of faith! Thank you, Brett!

TO OUR LORD AND SAVIOR, Jesus Christ, for planting the vision for this book and our ministry, we thank you from the bottom of our hearts. We know every idea, ounce of energy and determination, and door opened were solely provided by your love and grace. We are thankful you can read our hearts because mere words cannot fully express our gratitude.

Contents

Preface

WE'D BEEN DATING SEVERAL MONTHS when our decluttering journey unknowingly began. Lindon was explaining to Sherry how he'd arrived where he was in life. At the age of forty-three, he never anticipated being divorced, living in an apartment without cable or even a phone, and working a desk job for a fraction of what he had once earned. This hadn't been his plan and, clearly, it was nowhere close to what he'd envisioned for his life.

Sherry wasn't where she thought she'd be either. She was twice divorced, single for almost nine years, and raising two sons on her own. This scenario was not the stuff her dreams were made of—obviously.

We weren't complaining, mind you, just reflecting and sharing. We started discussing that while there was much we didn't have, there was certainly a lot we did. We had our health, amazing kids, suitable places to live, friends, and a growing relationship with each other. In the midst of difficult life setbacks and unrealized dreams, we both felt rich beyond compare.

The conversation surrounding what we did have led to a discussion about material possessions. We agreed that most of what we had was far more than we truly needed. Sherry had a four-bedroom house and, while it was comfortable, Lindon's two-bedroom apartment felt just as comfortable and far less overwhelming. There was less to clean, less to heat and cool, and less to manage in general. Less felt like more.

[*Sherry*] As I was sharing my thoughts with Lindon, he admitted that he felt the same way. He wasn't crazy about apartment living, but he acknowledged the past year had taught him valuable lessons—lessons he might not have learned had he still been surrounded by the things of his past. He'd lived with tremendous excess and, while that wasn't necessarily shameful, the experience of living much more modestly had made an impact. He wanted a simpler life with more freedom. It inspired him to think differently about the future and the choices he planned to make when he had the chance.

[*Lindon*] I explained to Sherry how I came to realize all of this. One day my friend Fred paid me a visit in my near-empty home. We were sitting on the living room couch, which was borrowed from the dogs and had recently been drug inside from the garage. I was newly separated after twenty-plus years of marriage, and the bulk of all I had owned was gone. In fact, my eight-year-old TV sat atop the only other stick of furniture left to my name. I told Fred how after living with close to nothing for just a few months, I found it didn't bother me as much as I'd anticipated. In fact, I found it very liberating. I joked that I could do "something with nothing" and referred to my decorating style as "American Minimalist." It wasn't by choice that I found myself in that situation, but it was my choice to make the most of what I had and learn from it. It had taken three months to turn the corner emotionally and an additional three months to be set free completely from the past—a personal journey that I'll share more about later.

A light bulb went off for both of us at the same moment. We started talking about how people can get bogged down not only by material things, but by negative clutter that invades every area of our lives. Our relationships, finances, kids, jobs, health, and spiritual wellbeing are all adversely impacted by the unnecessary and harmful stuff we accumulate and hang onto—physically, emotionally, and otherwise. This clutter had gripped each of us and held us back from the freedom to enjoy what we really felt called to—ministry. In the past, we'd each been involved with ministry but never to the degree that our hearts desired. It was a defining moment.

What happened next felt as if we were in a movie on fast forward. The ideas were flying and we were furiously writing notes trying to keep up with them; everything came together so quickly. We were brainstorming on what it would take to declutter each of these areas so we would be free as a couple for God's calling. We were ready to be ready!

As we formulated our decluttering concept and put it in motion, the results were amazing. We knew we were on the right track and felt a crazy excitement to share what we were doing with others, hence the birth of *Declutter Now!* Since the moment we began, our enthusiasm hasn't waned a bit, in fact, it has grown by leaps and bounds.

The Two of Us

Through *Declutter Now!* we bring to you, combined, almost a century of living. We were both extremely independent and responsible kids, worked since our early teen years, yearned to grow up too quickly, moved multiple times as youngsters, married too young, survived divorce, and raised wonderful children. We don't argue over religion or politics because our positions are often similarly aligned, and we enjoy the same hobbies and interests. Talk about bookends, right? Well, not so fast…

While Lindon has traveled extensively, held positions from every end of the job spectrum you can imagine, and was willing to take risks, Sherry has been more of a homebody, content with the security of a steady job for the past sixteen years. She's lived in the same square mile area for the past twenty-four years, took comfort in her routines, and always colored inside the lines. Lindon was raised as a Christian and accepted the Lord at the tender age of six. With almost no spiritual influence, Sherry didn't realize anything was missing until after the birth of her oldest son, Ryan; then she sought God out with a passion and was saved at age twenty-one. So, even though there is much we share, our individual experiences and personalities lend a different attitude and viewpoint to most discussions. As a proverb says, two strands are better than one! Unified, we offer a comprehensive approach and are able to speak from a richer perspective, chock full of double the life experience.

When we married, we blended our families and gained a couple of daughters-in-law along the way. The four-bedroom home that Sherry owned has been decluttered, and we've made significant progress in decluttering other areas of our lives as well. It's a process and there's still work to be done, but we are well on our way to freeing up our hearts, minds, bodies, and souls so we can obtain the true joy and freedom needed to serve God and those around us—the freedom to give all that we have.

Less can truly be more, and we feel abundantly blessed in a way each of us has never known. We pray that, through this journey, you too will find true joy and freedom in living the decluttered life that God intended for you.

Introduction

WELCOME TO THE FIRST COMPREHENSIVE book on decluttering! What we are presenting will revolutionize the way you navigate through every area of your life, bring you unprecedented joy and freedom, and cultivate a new enthusiasm in your walk with Christ. We're genuinely excited you have this book in your hands. It doesn't matter whether it simply caught your attention while you were perusing your local bookstore or it was a gift from a well-meaning person in your life. Perhaps you know us personally and are reading this under sheer duress and obligation (we'll show you how to avoid that in the future). Whatever the reason, we pray the words will speak to your heart, and you'll come away from our time together feeling it was worth every second.

When most of us think of removing junk, we often isolate the thought to only physical tasks such as cleaning out the garage or a closet. It has become big business and there are now companies specializing in nothing more than removing clutter and organizing space more efficiently. Networks devote millions of dollars from their budgets to produce shows that address cleaning out your home, space efficiency, and exposing people with hoarding problems. Obviously there's an interest in decluttering and a need for it.

Our theory is that cleaning out clutter shouldn't just be reserved for material items. We're going to challenge you to build upon the decluttering concept and use it to transform EVERY area of your life—your heart, mind, body, soul, as well as your home.

When you declutter, you let go of the unnecessary, and letting go makes room for you to consider the next step. Do you want to leave the space empty? Should you fill it with something more useful? More efficient? More pleasurable? Now consider what could happen if you applied this process to your relationships or finances? How about with your kids or in your careers? With your mental or physical health? What if you remove harmful clutter from each part of your life? Are you starting to grasp the potential for total life change? How much room would be left for healthy, positive living? Just like a music CD that's completely full, you have to remove the unwanted songs before you can add the new favorites you're dying to hear. We'll share with you how decluttering your life will bring freedom and amazing opportunities that reach far beyond just your garage or closet.

"The ability to simplify means to eliminate the unnecessary so that the necessary may speak"

(Hans Hofmann).

Each of us has our own set of personal challenges. We can get complacent and immerse ourselves in mundane routines and bad habits. We find false security in our stuff and covet what we shouldn't. We keep company with the wrong people for the wrong reasons. We eat for comfort and use artificial means to numb us. We hold on to negative and painful feelings. Think about all of the unnecessary things we gather from these behaviors and choices—stagnant lifestyles, needless and excessive stuff, financial debt, obligation, guilt, extra weight, anger, hurt, discontentment, addictions; the list is endless. Consider the negative influence these have on the quality of our lives and how they impact our relationship with God. Remove the unnecessary so the necessary has room to surface and prepare to be amazed at the blessings which will emerge.

You'll find we use the word freedom often in this book. It's the crux of what we pray you will receive. Freedom allows you to step back, catch your breath, focus, reorganize, and get control. Freedom empowers you to broaden your vision and see the bigger picture. You'll have choices and can operate without guilt or obligation. This is foreign to most people, but with a little effort and determination, you can and will.

Freedom itself brings a whole host of benefits, but most importantly, you'll be blessed by having more time and energy to choose God, more time and energy to do the work he's created you to do. This is truly the heart of the journey. There generally isn't a correlation made between decluttering and a relationship with God, but we believe there should be. Have you ever felt too busy for God? Too overwhelmed, rushed, or unfocused? These challenges will seriously impede your walk with Christ. Since decluttering removes what you don't need and gives you more of what you do, it only makes sense your spiritual journey will benefit too. There is hope, but there's also work to be done!

We've each made more bad decisions than we care to recall because we felt bondage to the unnecessary, unimportant, and harmful. Why in the world do we do this? What benefit comes in compromising our own wellbeing for anything that adversely affects our lives? We'll share our thoughts on the root of destructive patterns and offer step-by-step advice how to free yourself from these burdens and never look back.

You're probably familiar with the saying, "You don't know what you're missing!" Keep this adage handy and at your disposal. Perhaps write it on an index card and use it as the bookmark for this book. If the going gets tough, remind yourself of this over and over again. You may not have yet experienced the freedom decluttering brings, but it's just around the corner, and you truly have no idea the unbelievable joy you're missing.

If you become drained by the truths you're uncovering or are struggling to keep up with the tasks you want to accomplish, don't feel guilty about taking a short break. It's perfectly okay to pause; there's a lot to absorb and do. Perhaps you make tremendous progress decluttering in one area but your excitement causes you to lose focus about moving on to the next. It's okay to delight in your success; you deserve it. Just don't stall permanently! The value of the decluttering process is rooted in the comprehensive nature of the material, and total success will only be realized if you follow through to the end.

We believe it takes an all-inclusive approach to renovate the whole person. As with a home remodel, you may have to work on one room at a time, but the project isn't complete until all the rooms are finished. While you may find joy in your gorgeous new kitchen, when you leave that room and step into your bathroom with the yellowing, curled vinyl, paint-chipped walls, and rusted bathtub, your joy will quickly diminish. Decluttering one area is better than none, but that alone is not enough to overcome the clutter left in other parts of your life.

Undoubtedly you won't agree with everything we say, and we know that not every piece of advice will be helpful or applicable to your situation. We encourage you to dissect the information and choose what works for you. Sherry often refers to this as her "Personal Stew." Gather bits and pieces of helpful ingredients from different sources you trust and respect, and put it together to make your own unique recipe.

Our goal is to bring enlightenment: a fresh perspective and awareness to any behaviors and situations which may be hindering and hurting you. We'll then motivate you to take action and offer extensive advice and practical tips to guide you in working through the clutter. If, while you're decluttering, you uncover a serious problem which requires additional help, we strongly recommend you seek additional resources. Whether that requires enlisting the assistance of family and friends, meeting with your pastor, seeking counseling or medical help, joining support groups, or a combination of all of the above, we encourage you to be diligent in your effort toward total healing and restoration.

First Things First

We'll begin in the first chapter with the physical clutter in our lives. This section didn't make it to the front by chance. While sometimes difficult to do, this is the area where you're most likely to see easy, almost instant results. Use your early success as a confidence builder and motivator for the other decluttering areas where achieving your goals may be more emotionally taxing or require a slower-paced, gradual climb.

We strive to bring an understanding and compassionate angle to our discussions, and offer sound advice, encouragement, and support. There aren't any magical solutions or get-rich-quick schemes. What we propose is a shift in your axis, a transformation in the way you think, act, and feel. This will take determination and effort. Our number one priority is that you uncover the hidden joy and freedom in your life, and we honestly believe if you give the ideas in *Declutter Now!* a legitimate shot and stick to it, you will achieve success. Do it for yourself, your spouse, your kids, your friends and, most importantly, for God.

Chapter 1

Having Everything You've Ever Wanted (by Letting Go of Everything You Never Needed)

"Then he said to them, 'Watch out! Be on your guard against all kinds of greed; a man's life does not consist in the abundance of his possessions.'"

(Luke 12:15)

IN THE PARABLE OF THE rich fool, Christ warns about the "more is better" mentality, contradicting what today's society generally promotes. We're going to show how LESS can actually be more: more gratifying, more satisfying, more manageable, and more freeing. Basically, more of all the good stuff and all that is really needed. Jesus challenges us to think beyond our earthly possessions and spend our time preparing for eternity. We aren't to be consumed with the material things acquired here on earth. If we kept this at the forefront of our decisions and acted accordingly, imagine how differently our lives could play out.

Welcome to the first step of your decluttering experience. This chapter is far more than just a "how to clean out your house" instructional guide. In fact, cleaning your home is just the beginning. We suspect many of you are wincing at this point, but it's not that bad! You'll find the comprehensive aspects of what we share so far-reaching (and hopefully insanely inspiring) that your entire perspective on your home and possessions will take on new meaning.

Jesus tells us in Matthew 6:21, "For where your treasure is, there your heart will be also." What are your treasures? What is truly most important to you? You might have a TV in every room, a brand new toy hauler in your side yard, and enough designer outfits to single-handedly clothe half the US, but when asked what your true treasure is, your response would likely not be one of these items. We guess it would be more along the lines of spending time with your spouse, enjoying your children, helping someone in need, or being on vacation in a place that you love visiting. There are other responses that might similarly qualify, but we're willing to go out on a limb and speculate your true treasure isn't found in a 60-inch HD TV or a designer watch; neither is ours. So, if that's the case, then why oh why do we clutter our space and lives with so much "stuff" that has nothing to do with the true joy of our hearts?

Here's another example of clutter to ponder. Have you ever walked into someone's home and wondered why they live in such a cluttered state? There are piles of things on countertops, the dining room table, and the staircase that haven't been touched in months, not to mention the garage, which is filled to the ceiling with storage bins and junk. There is disarray and possibly filth. (People who don't *clean out* clutter rarely clean *around* or *under* clutter.) The house may feel depressing, dark, and suffocating. What leads to this kind of environment? Is it upbringing? Laziness? Lifestyle? Lack of concern? Lack of time?

Obviously there can be many factors that can precipitate these situations, but we believe there are three major underlying instigators: clinging to the past, the more is better mindset, and allowing your life to control you.

Clinging to the Past

Clinging to the past can be at fault when you just can't part with anything. *Everything* has a special meaning, a wonderful memory, or an indispensable purpose—absolutely everything. You know your excuses, which are probably racing to your defense right now. You keep collecting and accumulating, all the while never clearing anything out to make room for new additions, so the clutter keeps growing. You continue adding to the piles, but you have every justification down pat and you're a genius at rationalizing each purchase.

If this is your situation, you're not alone. We understand your possessions have meaning and purpose, and we aren't trying to minimize their significance to you. What we propose, however, is establishing a healthy perspective. We'll share useful ideas on how to manage this type of challenge. Keep reading!

Operating in the More is Better Mindset

The "more is better" mindset is a biggie and is fueled by a variety of issues. Do you fear not having enough or not being able to replace the things you do have should they break or get worn out? Sherry will share with you her personal understanding of this deep-rooted fear. It can be overcome! Acknowledgement is a big part of the battle and, if you're willing to do that, we can help. Do you find that it's often all about *acquiring* things? We use the term "acquisition man" (or woman) to reference people who are consumed with nothing but the acquisition. Sadly, they often never really enjoy all that they amass. Do you have a need to compete with the Joneses? Do you find out what everyone else has before deciding what you're going to get? Do you let other people and families become the standard to meet or surpass for your own purchases or decisions?

If this is the case, you might realize deep inside that there's a problem, but on the surface it just feels too good to correct. Even if it doesn't feel all that good, you're so caught up in the acquisition merry-go-round that it's just easier to stay on board rather than jump off and make changes. What may seem easier initially can have the most damaging results later. Don't fret! God can heal you from these distractions and hindrances. Keep reading!

Allowing Your Life to Run You

Your schedule is so busy there isn't time to breathe. Any change of plans throws you into a tailspin because there's no wiggle room. Your front door is a turnstile and you aren't home long enough to tackle the piles that grow as you dump and run. When you finally have an hour or two free, you're busy doing damage control (a.k.a. trying to catch up). Are you suffering from a lack of time, structure, and energy so nothing gets taken care of properly? Everything suffers from a half-hearted effort producing a lackluster result. This lifestyle will not only drain you physically and emotionally, but most assuredly derail any chance for physical decluttering success.

Feeling burdened or convicted yet? Good! No, we aren't being callous, but we're excited for you to recognize the areas that need adjustment or even a complete overhaul. It's a start! Wouldn't it be nice to have all that wasted and misdirected energy back? You can and it's not that hard to reclaim. Imagine the possibilities! If you're still with us and haven't slammed the book shut yet, don't stop now. Help is on the way. Keep reading!

The Common Denominator

When you contemplate the three main instigators that lead to a life of physical clutter, there's one factor they all have in common: bondage. They keep you chained to the past and trapped in the present with no ability to have vision or excitement for the future. Where is your motivation to embrace all that is to come if you can't think beyond the past you are stuck in or the present that horribly overwhelms you? Before you can declutter, you have to uncover the underlying reasons behind your clutter and come to terms with what's holding you back. Only then will you stand a chance in conquering the ties that bind. Declutter from the inside out. Make space in your mind and heart to enjoy the present and look forward to the future. Figure out what has a hold on you and make a decision to start fearlessly conquering it now! This journey may be as simple as a light-bulb moment and a commitment to start a fresh new day in a fresh new way, or it might require painful soul searching and even counseling. Whatever the case, remember, "And my God will meet all your needs according to his glorious riches in Christ Jesus" (Phil. 4:19). There is nothing to be afraid of and everything to gain.

We're going to give you practical advice in getting started and coach you every step of the way. As we work through the physical decluttering together, we pray that you'll find encouragement, answers, and motivation. It'll come together as we start to discuss what to do with what you have.

Following Jesus' Lead

God never intended us to be bogged down with worldly possessions. Look at Jesus' example. He wasn't spreading the gospel through the countryside with a moving van following him every step of the way. In fact, it was quite the opposite. He and his disciples traveled quite light. Their focus was on sharing God's word and ministering to the masses, not on acquiring possessions or showing them off. The idea of being physically decluttered is so much more than a once-a-year spring cleaning. Follow Jesus' lead and embrace a new way of life and a different mindset that will benefit you every day of the year.

So, how do you start? Where in the world, or in your house, do you begin? The reason we began with this action chapter is the sheer idea of instant gratification. We want everything quickly; we need everything yesterday. The drive-thru should not take more than a few minutes (isn't it "fast" food?), our internet better perform at lightning speed, and we expect instant access to people at all times. With this in mind, starting with a task that produces immediate results seemed to be the perfect springboard. The sense of fulfillment and accomplishment you glean from physically decluttering will pave the way and encourage you in other areas that may take a bit more time and effort before you realize progress. As you work through each step and every chapter, you'll start to see the puzzle fit together, and you'll obtain the level of understanding and proficiency that is key for total success. Get started! It's not as hard as you expect.

Project Management

In order to efficiently manage your decluttering project, start a list. Sherry is a huge list maker, and while this may not be the preferred method for everyone, give it a try. Grab a clipboard and a pen and pretend you are a foreman surveying a jobsite. List all of the rooms and areas that need to be decluttered and be specific. Consider everything—shelves, drawers, closets, etc. Walk around your home, inside and out, and jot down notes as you encounter areas that need attention. Don't hold back. This is your Declutter Dream List.

After your list is complete, log each item with an "A" for the most important tasks, "B" for tasks of moderate priority, or "C" for the least of your worries. Then order, within each letter group, the importance of the area to be decluttered. For instance, A1, A2, A3, B1, B2, B3, and so on. This method can take overwhelming tasks and make them feel manageable almost instantly.

When you begin, start with A1 and concentrate only on A1. Don't get disheartened by all that is left on the list, but rather just focus on the task at hand. The most important element is to actually begin: step over the line and start. Set time aside each day or week to work on your list, even if it's only fifteen or twenty minutes at a pop. You'll be surprised at how much can be accomplished in relatively short order when you have a plan and are disciplined to make it happen. You might even find there are days you get into a groove and spend five times as much time on your project as you had planned.

As you work through each area, you'll ask yourself a thousand times, "What should I keep and what should I part with?" There are more options available than just tossing your stuff, and we present some guidelines and suggestions below to help you make decisions you can live with. Sort as you work through the clutter. Pretty soon you'll be an old pro.

As each area is decluttered, you'll be amazed at how good it feels when you step back and admire your accomplishment. When your vacuum fits in the closet and you can actually shut the door, or when you can open the kitchen drawer without it getting stuck on the junk, you'll get what we're saying. And by all means, continue to read ahead while you work on decluttering your home. There is so much that can be done concurrently, and the more you practice, the more natural it'll become.

Set the Cut

How many items did you find tucked in drawers or stuck in the top of closets that you didn't even remember were there (e.g., everything that is shoved in the back of the dreaded junk drawer)? How many things have you moved from house to house without ever using or perhaps without even knowing what was in the boxes you moved from the garage? We've done this in the past but no more! Choose a time frame that's comfortable for you and if you've not used an item within that pre-determined limit, lose it! And before you get any funny ideas, a five- or ten-year period is not quite what we had in mind. We suggest something more along the lines of six months or a year. If you haven't looked at it or touched it in that length of time, chances are another year will go by and you'll still be in exactly the same boat. What's the advantage in surrounding yourself with unused things that just take up space and collect dust? We've got some better ideas on what to do with these things. Commit to changing your course of inaction and inattention, and embark on a fresh, new journey.

What to Do with It All

After you've gone through all the areas on your list and have amassed the extra and unnecessary items, you'll have to decide what to do with what you have. Cleaning out your stuff is only the first step in the decluttering journey. Actually getting it all, or at least most of it OUT of your house is the key. Some things may be worthy of nothing more than being tossed in the garbage can, but there will be lots of candidates for either a yard sale or donation. Focus on the end result and stay motivated to see this through to fruition.

Could you use "free" money from a yard sale for a much needed home repair or to purchase something your child might require for the upcoming sports or band season? Maybe you'd like to put the money towards financing a family outing or vacation? Do you have a credit card that should be paid off, or at least one that would benefit from an additional principal payment? It's such a sense of accomplishment when you're able to recycle the unnecessary so that, without giving up anything valuable or important, you not only have cash in hand for something special, but you've decluttered your home in the process. Look toward the end result and use it to motivate you.

Perhaps a yard sale is not for you and you would simply prefer to donate to needy causes? "Sell your possessions and give to the poor" (Luke 12:33). Jesus instructs us over and over again to be generous and give. What a perfect opportunity to be obedient! No matter where you live, every community has those in need. You may even know friends or family members in a tough spot or in a different life-stage who would appreciate the things that are no longer useful to you. Clothing, shoes, jackets, blankets, toys, games, kitchenware, and furniture can always find thankful homes.

"If there is a poor man among your brothers in any of the towns of the land that the Lord your God is giving you, do not be hardhearted or tightfisted toward your poor brother. Rather be openhanded and freely lend him whatever he needs" (Deut. 15:7-8). God doesn't instruct us to limit our giving to monetary donations or items that are easy to part with. He says "whatever." He wants us to give freely wherever the need is. Look for creative ways to help and don't necessarily wait to be asked. Some of the best opportunities will pass you by if you aren't proactive about initiating your giving. Look for needs, offer the help, and go above and beyond. When you think about the excess you have and then think of people who have great need, doesn't it just make sense to share? Everyone wins.

Ahhhhh......RESULTS!

Words on paper can't adequately convey the adrenaline rush you'll feel once you start making some real progress. Give it a try and see for yourself. When you walk through your house and see your closets cleaned out, when the space around you feels airy and organized, when you have a few extra bucks in your pocket and the ability to decide where you want to spend it, and when you see the faces of those grateful for the help you've lent, you'll then begin to understand the basic purpose behind this first foundational step. It sounds simple. Clean your stuff out and get rid of it. Actually doing it, though, doing it now and doing it well, will set your pace and start you on the right track.

Another benefit to this type of decluttering was brought to our attention while we were presenting to a small group in our church. Brett, our group leader, was gracious to allow us to teach a miniseries based on the curriculum we wrote from book chapters that weren't even finished yet. Our friends in small group became our personal guinea pigs, and we knew that Brett's good name, and that of his small group, were at stake. We wondered if he was as worried as we were. Or at least as worried as Sherry was. Thankfully, we can say that not only did all the group members survive, they seemed to enjoy and benefit from the lessons, and so did we. We learned a great deal from their feedback and insight.

During the first week of our series while we were discussing this chapter, one of the group members, Patti, mentioned that both her parents had recently passed away within six months of each other. The past year had been an emotional rollercoaster and a difficult time in her life, as you might imagine. After her parents died, she and her siblings had the monumental task of sorting through an entire house, a very big house, full of belongings. Her parents had lived there for over forty years! She entertained us with stories about the mass quantity of items that her parents had accumulated during this time. There were twelve of this kind of tool and seven of that. Patti found massive multiples of everything. The kitchen was no exception and there were more clothes than anyone could wear in a lifetime.

Although Patti loved her parents dearly and wasn't upset by this herculean task, she was also convinced that had her parents decluttered along the way, the task would not have been nearly as time consuming nor overwhelming, and she would have been grateful not to have had this undertaking. This really made us think. Do we want to burden our children with having to declutter our lives for us after we're gone? Absolutely not! When you think about it in those terms, it doesn't seem fair, does it? We bet you'll agree with us that the simple answer to this question is no. Thanks, Patti, for sharing your story. Without a doubt, you've already made a profound difference in lots of lives: those that will be more motivated to declutter, if for no other reason than on behalf of their children, and the children who will not be as burdened by the task.

Care is Key

We acknowledge and empathize that a difficult aspect of this undertaking is parting with items that elicit fond memories or have important family and personal value. We encourage you to evaluate each item individually. It's easy to just start collecting memorabilia or family heirlooms and not give much thought to what you're actually gathering and tucking away. We aren't suggesting you throw out items that are near and dear to your heart, but we encourage you to take action and do something positive with what you come across.

For instance, do you have items that you have meant to have fixed, refurbished, or cleaned so that they can be displayed or used? Then by all means, get it done! If the item is truly that special, it makes far more sense to put it out where you can appreciate or use it, rather than having it just take up space in a box tucked away in the corner of the attic. Perhaps you have some family heirlooms that you were planning on passing down. If the person you are gifting to is old enough to be responsible, then why not share it now and allow them to enjoy it today? And if they are not old enough to care for or appreciate it yet, then give it to their parents for safe keeping. Whatever it takes, just get it out of *your* house! OK, we are being a bit facetious here, but you get the idea.

The same concept applies to photos. Do you have hundreds of pictures stored in boxes that never get viewed? We are guilty of this as well and are working on taking our own advice. Choose your favorite photos, frame them and display them so that you can enjoy them. As with our suggestion in the previous paragraph, why not make now a good time to pass along some of the photos that are meaningful to others? Just because they're important, doesn't mean you have to be the keeper.

WAIT! If you are already balking at the paragraph you just read, that is natural. It *is* really difficult to part with family photos. That is why most of us keep so many pictures, even ones that are poor quality—they seem to represent family and friends. So here is your way out of being the keeper of boxes of photos you can't bring yourself to part with: save them in a much more compact form. Input them electronically onto a computer disc. Photo shops and some drug store chains have machines that walk you through how to do it. They also will do it for you at a reasonable price. If you're computer savvy, you can scan pictures from your printer into your hard drive and put them on a CD or flash drive. You could also upload them into a digital picture frame which holds hundreds of photos and plays them like a slide show. You will still have some decisions to make in the decluttering process. Refuse to scan or upload out-of-focus shots, duplicate or even similar poses—choose the best photo. When your photos are kept electronically, their footprint is tiny. Remember Patti's story; your heirs will thank you too.

Memories are special. We're not minimizing memories or promoting a heartless approach. We are simply suggesting you become selective and intentional. Keep the mementos that mean the most, but by all means use or display them and keep their importance alive. After you've saved the crème de la crème for yourself, be diligent in parting with what's left over. Where the items go is not necessarily vital. Whether to a family member, friend, museum, or charitable organization, the key here is to put it in the hands of someone who will use, love, and appreciate it, just as we hope you will do with the things you hang onto.

Fear in Disguise

Another challenge you may face is parting with items that you believe bring you comfort. We sometimes have a false or warped sense of security. Do you feel more secure being surrounded by an abundance of the same item? Do you live in fear of "not having enough" or "not being able to replace this." Do these concerns influence the decisions you make? For Sherry, this was particularly true.

[*Sherry*] It may sound irrational, but as a single parent, I stored dozens and dozens of blankets in my home. New ones, old ones, big ones, small ones, every kind you could imagine. The thought of my kids ever being cold was so disturbing that I made sure to have enough blankets on hand so that could never happen. I was on a tight, fixed income, and I was terrified that I might not be able to afford what we needed, so I simply kept collecting and storing anything that came my way. I parted with nothing! You have no idea the stockpile of jackets I also kept on hand, although admittedly, I could rarely convince my boys to actually wear one. Back to the blankets... How many did the boys and I really need? Maybe a couple of spares to keep on hand, but more than that was total overkill—especially since we lived in Phoenix, Arizona, where there are few days below 70 degrees! Looking back, I'm regretful because I know there were many children that could have benefited from the warmth of the blankets that were lying on the floor of my closets, but fear gripped my heart and I was in "protection" and "survival" mode.

We often stress the importance of moderation. It makes sense to have a spare or two of something for that just-in-case moment but, in general, it's counterproductive to operate with the fear of too many "what ifs" and go overboard. This mode of operation will rob you of much peace and joy. Admittedly, some things may be harder to replace than others, but there isn't much that can't, one way or the other, be replaced. Fear is a restrictive state of mind that will suppress your freedom and strangle any opportunity you might otherwise have had to live by faith. Don't allow this to control you. Our friend Roger says that fear and faith cannot co-exist. We believe this to be true. Which will you choose?

Sherry credits Lindon with being instrumental in working through this type of challenge in her life, although we will both attest that it got off to a rocky start.

[*Lindon*] Can you imagine someone crying real tears over parting with bags? While gathering items for our first decluttering yard sale, I assumed that Sherry was planning to sell the bulk of her twenty-two or so bags that were stuffed in the front closet. We're talking *all* sorts of bags—overnight bags, beach bags, day-trip bags. LOTS OF BAGS! To me, this seemed like a natural, harmless assumption, however, it was anything but that. It elicited a lot of very strong feelings from Sherry and none of them were good, at least not initially.

I, with all my charm and tact, suggested she keep the "nice new one," the key word being *one*. Sherry looked at me, completely offended, as if I'd just asked her to give up her firstborn son. I didn't understand that to Sherry these bags were some of the many things she'd gathered in her home that represented security and preparedness. She might need one of those bags someday and, if she parted with it, she might not have the money to replace it. It was just safer to keep them all. As a single parent with a single income, Sherry had been on a strict financial budget for years and operating in safe mode was natural and normal, even with bags.

Anything outside of that was frightening.

I can only imagine you reading this, shaking your head and thinking Sherry was being quite melodramatic over her bags. I guess it's safe to admit, now, I kind of did too! But at the time, how you do you think I felt? There I stood in the hallway by the closet, looking at Sherry with big tears welling up in her eyes, while her oldest son walked up and asked suspiciously, "Mom, what's wrong?" It was not a moment I want to repeat! The truth I learned, however, is the tears were not over the bags themselves but what they represented. Her house was somewhat cluttered, but to her it was just being ready for anything; she was being a responsible mom. It gave her comfort to know she was stocked up and there were fewer things that she might have to buy with her limited income. To her it made sense. She kept things around because it gave her a sense of having more. Unfortunately, *more* was clutter that allowed her fear to remain unchallenged and her faith to be stifled. There is zero room for trust or growth when operating in safe mode.

Are you beginning to see how this mindset can spill over into so many areas of your life and what a damaging effect it can have? It goes far beyond just the stuff. The stuff is a symptom, similar to what a fever is to an infection. It's merely the indicator that something is wrong, but it isn't the actual problem itself. Sherry finally did part with most of the bags and admitted that she experienced a great freeing. It got so much easier after that. I can now say with great pride there are just a few multipurpose bags in that dreaded front closet. My wife took a difficult first step, trusted, and set a paradigm that continues to serve us well. Oh, and I sure didn't mind the $25 we pocketed for selling the bags and the absence of them falling on my head every time I reached into the closet. Life is good.

To further elaborate, are you the kind of person that buys something only to rope it off and quarantine it because you are reticent to use it up? Are you fearful that while enjoying whatever it is, it may break from repeated use and you may never be able to replace it? Stop for a second and reread that! If you are guilty of this, did you see the red flags going up as you realized the absurdity of the question? When you actually think about it, is there any logic in this rationale at all? If you buy it, isn't the point to use it and enjoy it? Heavens yes! If you are just going to stare at it, you might as well not spend any money on the item and leave it in the store where it belongs. Simply frequent the store and you can look at it there without spending a dime. Point made?

IT'S JUST STUFF!

[*Sherry*] I have adopted a saying that has saved me *tons* of angst and despair. It never failed that when I got something new, whether a vehicle, cell phone, sunglasses, *anything*, I'd invariably scratch, drop, or damage it within the first twenty-four hours. This was maddening and disappointing to say the least! After this happened repeatedly, it seemed to be far too coincidental not to mean something. I believe God speaks to us in a variety of ways, and I had a feeling this was definitely a message meant to get my attention. God impressed upon me: IT'S JUST STUFF! Say it out loud: IT'S JUST STUFF! It doesn't stand the test of fire, it's not going with you, and it doesn't determine your worth or happiness. IT'S JUST STUFF!

Oddly enough, Lindon has had much the same experience. His new 1984 Dodge suffered a scratch in the left front fender after owning it just three short weeks, and his new Ford truck was hit by a hockey puck also after just three weeks. Now when that first scratch happens, which it inevitably will, we just laugh and know it's God speaking to us with a sweet reminder of what's not so important after all.

As I write this, I'm chuckling at the timing. I had this conversation today in our kitchen with Katie, our daughter-in-law. Katie and Ryan are newlyweds and have had a ball setting up their home; everything has pretty much gone picture perfect. This is no surprise. They are both organized planners and conscientious shoppers. They just bought the perfect dinette set for their eat-in kitchen. Katie, not realizing the surface wasn't real wood, damaged the table top while trying to clean it with a wood cleaner. I could tell she felt bad. Furniture is expensive and this was their first set; it was barely days old. I'm sure she may have also been a little embarrassed to tell Ryan what happened. Katie is very down to earth and not caught up in material things, but I still have to believe she was bummed by what she'd done. I gave her my "it's just stuff" story and I could see the relief in her eyes as she related to the lesson I was sharing. While Katie already subscribed to this idea in theory, I think it was nice to hear it from someone who loves her dearly. Keep this in mind for someone in your circle who needs to be let off the hook for a mistake. Keep it in mind for yourself too! In the scheme of things, what really is important?

A favorite line from one of my pastors was, "I ain't never seen no hearse with a U-Haul behind it!" Puts things in perspective quickly, doesn't it? Enjoy what you have and use it to the fullest because it's not going with you anyway. It's all JUST STUFF!

Trust God

Fear and worry can permeate your life in the most unassuming ways. You may not initially understand how these seemingly insignificant tendencies can radically affect your life, but once you start to work through the decluttering process, it will become abundantly evident the tremendous impact they have. Where is your faith? Where is your belief that God will provide? We aren't saying to throw caution to the wind and make irresponsible or foolish decisions, but there's a difference between that and existing in a stagnant life, suffocated with bondage. God has your back and when you are in need, he will provide. Take a no-regrets approach. Enjoy what you have. Embrace it and make the most of it. God wouldn't allow you to have it in the first place if he didn't want your life to be enriched by it. Remember, life is not a dress rehearsal. You get one shot, so enjoy it and do it right.

House of Refuge

Your decluttering process will provide you freedom and peace of mind, the joy of knowing you have helped others, and some extra cash in your pocket. You'll also end up with some extra space. Leave that room open for relatives or friends in need of a place to stay. We know you're probably thinking "why the heck would I want to do that?" but stop the negativity. We're being totally serious! You can provide short-term help for those with an immediate need. Opening your home to others may be the key to opening doors in your own life. We've both always had the feeling that our home will be a "house of refuge." We often keep this in mind when discussing choices for the future. Don't get us wrong. We don't live every minute waiting for a busload of people to show up, nor is the house stocked with 500 rolls of toilet paper. We do, however, make an assertive effort to leave some wiggle room in our lives so that, if and when we're needed, we'll be in a position to help. In our chapter on relationships, we further discuss this concept and how to discern those in need of a hand up versus a hand out. Until then, just know that having the space available and being the arms of Jesus to those who truly need loving assistance will enrich your own life and theirs tenfold.

Empty Spaces

[*Lindon*] I have a friend, Eliel, who asked Sherry if we planned to have any more children. I overheard the question and we both answered with an emphatic, "NO!" at exactly the same time. Eliel knows we have a four-bedroom house and our last child was exiting shortly. He was inquiring what our plans were for the extra space. We laughed because we already had our office, workout room, and guest room all planned. Eliel proceeded to share, ever so sincerely, that God doesn't like empty spaces and he'll fill up any you leave open. Eliel told us not to be so sure that kids weren't in our future line-up because, after all, it was up to God and not us. He deduced this from a few unused bedrooms? His comments have haunted us ever since, but they've also inspired us to ponder his rationale.

If we leave some empty space, both physically and in our hearts and heads, we allow God room to work within our lives and grow us. Make sense? If we keep everything filled up, what room is available for God? We essentially squeeze him out and hinder his ability to work in our lives. Ironically, it ended up that the house was kid-free for fourteen days. Fourteen days! REALLY? One of the extra bedrooms was filled up when our youngest, Devin, moved back home. We are still remodeling the other rooms and plan to do so quickly before God decides to fill them up with other boomerang kids or who knows who else. All kidding aside, some open and empty space is a good thing. It affords you wiggle room in decision making, which is another road to freedom, and it leaves space for God to enter in. Can you see God smiling about this prospect?

Don't Compound Your Clutter

Decluttering and making space means you actually discard, give away, or otherwise remove the unnecessary. Decluttering *doesn't* mean moving all your junk to a storage unit to sit, rotting away, and costing you money. This is adding insult to injury by compounding physical clutter with financial clutter. Don't get caught in the "Storage Unit Rut"! In America, with average rental storage fees ranging from $40 to $250 / month, our advice is save yourself $2,000 / year and make $500+ on a yard sale. Invest the money you make in your future, not in storing items you'll never use or enjoy!

Lindon speaks from experience on this subject. He was the last child of six and he'll tell you that growing up, and having moved twelve times before high school graduation, brought about some unique challenges. He lived with parents who, at one time, had three separate storage units in two states as they moved from place to place. Look at it this from the financial investment perspective. Three storage units at $180 each, multiplied by fifteen years, equates to about $97,200 that his parents wasted on storing stuff—stuff that ultimately was trashed, given away, or sold in a yard sale. Perhaps their example is on the extreme side, but it speaks to what big business the storage unit industry is. Think about it: if they're making money, someone is losing it.

Brainstorm for a second and imagine what Lindon's parents could have done with that money—$100,000 invested and spent wisely can go a long way. Think about the waste in storing stuff they didn't need to begin with. It's so unfortunate.

Of course there is a time and place for utilizing a storage unit. You may need a place to temporarily store your furniture while your house is being built. If you have a legitimate short-term need, then do what you have to do. However, if you are throwing money away month after month to store stuff you'll never use and don't need, your decluttering efforts must move on to the self-storage unit today! Stop wasting money. USE IT OR LOSE IT! College educations could be paid for and retirement funds created by eliminating your storage unit fees. Who would have *thunk*?

Now, with all this being said, if you do have a valid need to store some things, consider a storage shed? It'll be a one-time purchase that'll pay for itself in three to six months of storage unit fees, and will save you money each month thereafter. The shed will be on your property and at your immediate disposal. We, in fact, just purchased one and have had so much fun filling it up. Yes, we did say filling it up! ALL stuff is not BAD stuff. We've loaded it with our lawn care machines and tools, holiday decoration containers, and garage items. We've emptied our garage so that both of our vehicles now fit inside; they are more secure and their paintjobs get occasional reprieves from the scorching Arizona sun.

Positive Pointers

Once you get decluttered, it's a good idea to stay that way. Aside from the obvious steps to accomplish that, here are just a few tips to keep you on the right track.

Ward Off the Worldly

Keeping up with the Joneses is a noteworthy culprit. We live in a society where everyone wants it bigger, faster, and more elaborate. While this, in and of itself, can promote damaging shopaholic tendencies, many people are also obsessed with one-upping what their neighbor, co-worker, or family member has. A few times in our lives we've each fallen prey to this destructive thinking, but overall it hasn't been one of our top ten problems. We've seen the damage, though, done to those around us. Remember we mentioned the term "acquisition man." Often these acquisitions are empty. They rarely bring happiness or fulfillment. As soon as one purchase is made, you're off to the races to make the next one, never having even enjoyed the first.

People own expensive and complicated cell phones, electronics, and gadgets with features they never utilize. They usually don't even know how to fully operate what they've got. They just own it in order to say they do. A gadget for one fourth of the price with only the features they use would have sufficed, but that wouldn't cut it for keeping up with the Joneses. *What sense does this make? What kind of thinking leads to this hollow existence?* These are questions only you can answer, but we implore you to dig deep and make peace with the underlying driving force. The Apostle John speaks strongly against this type of behavior:

> "Do not love the world or anything in the world. If anyone loves the world, the love of the Father is not in him. For everything in the world—the cravings of sinful man, the lust of his eyes and the boasting of what he has and does—comes not from the Father but from the world. The world and its desires pass away, but the man who does the will of God lives forever."
>
> (1 John 2:15-17)

Could John have been any clearer? He is speaking not only of material things in the external sense but also of the people we associate with, the places we go, and the activities we enjoy. John includes internal qualities, such as our cravings, lusts, and boasts that will trip us up. In many cases, as with keeping up with the Joneses, one can easily and quickly lead to the other. Make an assertive effort to be on guard and to resist worldliness in any form.

There is something to be said for making purchases because you need the item or even simply because you want it, but make sure it is for your reasons and they are legitimate. Why spend your money on something your neighbor wanted? Doesn't that sound ridiculous? Most likely you don't need it, so it'll just be one more item to take up and clutter space. When you let go of an insecure, competitive spirit, you let go of many negative forces that are positioned to bring you down. Life alone has plenty of curveballs which you have no power over. Why not rid your life of the problems that are within your control to discard? It's a choice: your choice.

The Turnstile

And speaking of control, how many of you have lives that are spiraling completely out of control? While we may not have been able to speak from a deep desire to keep up with the Joneses, Sherry can speak to living a life that was running her. We cover a good portion of this in the chapter regarding children, but even without kids, one can still fall prey to doing too much and over-committing. Do you feel like your front door is a turnstile? Are you constantly running in and out, never staying long enough to enjoy your home or tend to chores? You run in, dump off stuff from work, run out, run back in, drop off some bags from the store, run out, run in, and crash in bed. We can get so busy that we fail to leave wiggle room in between our things to do, places to go, and people to see. Make a point to leave yourself time at home to catch up on the piles that accumulate from your busy day-to-day routine. Make time to declutter regularly on a much smaller daily scale so that your home will stay clutter-free indefinitely.

Now some of you obstinate types are already countering, "What's it to you if I do a bunch of smaller decluttering versus a huge declutter task less often?" We understand that people have different styles of attacking projects, but logistically speaking, if you choose to just do large decluttering projects once in a great while, you lose all the benefits of enjoying a decluttered home in between these efforts. It defeats the entire premise if the clutter is constantly growing around you. Keep it knocked down! "Who's the boss, applesauce?" You! Or you and your spouse. You are to set the pace, make the tough decisions, and maintain control over your own life.

Sensible Souvenirs

Here's a handy tip that we've taken to heart and put into practice often. When you go on vacation and feel inclined to bring home a souvenir from your trip, purchase something practical, something that you'll actually use and enjoy. We are in the process of making our backyard more festive for barbecues and gatherings. On each of the last few trips we have taken, we've collected souvenirs that will be great additions in decorating the patio of our dreams. By doing this, items that we would've purchased anyway now have a special memory attached. They don't take up any more space than if they'd come from a local store, but now they serve a dual purpose. It saved us money because we didn't purchase both a souvenir and decoration. It's a "two-for." There can be a lot of fun and pleasure using intentionality when making purchases, and you'll be pleasantly surprised what a big difference putting a few simple strategies in place can make.

Memory Book

We've also come up with a great way to store and preserve memories that doesn't take up much space, is fun to work on, and keeps memories alive. Lindon started our "Memory Book" on one of our first dates, and we've kept it going ever since. It started with just recording a memorable event, but it has become more of a living journal to us. Together, we write down all the details of a special time or time frame that we want to remember on a memory card and file the cards in plastic sleeves which are clipped into a small three-ring binder. It's so much fun jotting everything down and talking about where we went and what we did. We add lots of personal stories, opinions, and comments. There is no concern over neatness, spelling, or punctuation. We just write and have fun with it. Our Memory Book takes up minimal space and keeps the heart of our memories alive. From time to time when we peruse the pages and relive special moments, we are always amazed at the details already forgotten and grateful that they're preserved. This is much more meaningful to us than a bunch of dust collectors that would eventually end up in a yard sale like the one we are encouraging you to have.

You Made It!

Here we are at the end of your first Decluttering 101 lesson. We hope you're grasping the core of our belief system. Having some stuff is not the problem; we just want you to be extremely intentional about what you have and what you hold onto. Take quality over quantity. Ditch your fears so faith may abound. Use, enjoy, and take pleasure in what you have. Accumulate what is meaningful and beneficial; stay away from what isn't. Discard, sell, or donate the unimportant and unnecessary. Live with freedom and faith!

Most of us, during the worst times of our lives, have so much more than we need yet we fail to make sure we have the most important things that we desire, like time with God and our families. Take our advice to heart. You'll feel a sense of relief, freedom, peace, and confidence like you've never known. And through all of this, leave some space for God and seek his empowerment. Remember, even in projects that may not initially seem related to your personal walk with Christ, such as decluttering physical space and material things, there are opportunities to move closer to him. Be mindful of this in all you do, and God will so richly bless your journey that you'll know beyond a shadow of a doubt that less truly is more.

Chapter 2

Lovers, Lifesavers, Leeches, Losers, and Lost Causes

DID THE CHAPTER TITLE GET your attention? We hope so because that was our intention. This is a tough subject to broach and we wanted you to understand right out of the chute that we plan to hit it head on. Relationships, in many respects, are the most challenging to declutter. Instead of debating whether to give away an old pair of shoes or pass on the new ones you're dying to have, you're dealing with real people, their unique personalities, and a range of varied emotions. This is heart stuff and it can be tough.

Read the title again. Now stop for a moment and consider each category of people named. While you may not have previously considered labeling people in exactly these terms, if you did, we bet you'd know who falls into which label. Which people add beneficial, enriching, and positive elements to your life, and which ones tend to suck you dry or leave you with that "I wish I hadn't just wasted the last two hours of my life" feeling? Are your wheels spinning already? Often, we already know the answer; we just fail to make the connection. It takes a conscious effort to evaluate relationships and address the intangible in concrete terms.

When we first introduce these categories to people, we're never disappointed at how quickly their light goes on and names immediately come to mind. Even though the concept has proven to be incredibly relatable thus far, we still almost changed the title when we recently taught this section to our small group guinea pigs. We were afraid it sounded a bit too harsh or "un-Christian" and some might find it offensive. It's almost easier to write candidly to friends whom we don't know yet, than to personally present to those we do. Well, the discussion was going so well during the lesson that we felt confident enough to casually mention what the proposed title was. The group responded enthusiastically that they loved it. Really? We were a bit surprised, but pleasantly so! Thus, the name stayed and we made a commitment always to be true to our thoughts and feelings, whether we're behind the safety of our laptop, far out of earshot of our audience, or personally presenting in an intimate group setting.

Think about what decluttering your life means to you. Throughout the book, we're going to challenge you to think outside the box. While making physical room is critical to the entire process, making room in your life for the relationships that matter most and letting go of those that don't is just as crucial! This chapter is our favorite and especially meaningful because we've each made dramatic life changes which have benefited us tenfold. We speak to you from our hearts, from every experience that encouraged us to appreciate what we had that was good. And we'll share lessons learned making difficult choices when dealing with… lovers, lifesavers, leeches, losers, and lost causes.

Friend or Fraud?

"Elijah said to Elisha, 'Stay here; the LORD has sent me to Bethel.' But Elisha said, 'As surely as the Lord lives and as you live, I will not leave you.' So they went down to Bethel."

(2 Kings 2:2)

What exactly does "friend" mean to you? Friends can also include family members, but understand an important distinction. Being family doesn't necessitate an instant obligation for friendship. Like everything else, it's a choice. For the friends who come to mind first, do they bring you love and joy? Warmth and happiness? Do they support and encourage? Stand by your side? Do you feel better for knowing them? Learn from them? Is it like iron sharpening iron where they speak truth to you and bring perspective to your life? Do you offer the same to them? "As iron sharpens iron, so one man sharpens another" (Prov. 27:17). We pray you have a few of these precious gems in your circle.

Think about the other friends that are in your mix. Are there some that are always in need? They have problem after problem and are forever leeching off of you and depleting your time, energy, and resources. Are there any negative "professional victims," who are consumed with complaining but aren't willing or interested in actually making an effort for positive change? Do you remember in the movie *Ghostbusters* when the evil ones would "slime" their adversaries? It was a physical manifestation of what was going on in the spiritual realm. You can't always physically see when you're being slimed by those you know, but you sure can feel it.

The Bible tells us to choose our friends carefully and the Book of

Proverbs speaks strongly on this subject:

> *"A righteous man is cautious in friendship, but the*
> *way of the wicked leads them astray."*

(Prov. 12:26)

> *"He who walks with the wise grows wise, but a*
> *companion of fools suffers harm."*

(Prov. 13:20)

There are too many verses to list, but take some time reading through Proverbs and glean from the wise counsel given. Let God in, and he won't let you down!

Ditching the Drain

The reality is you probably have friends on both ends of the gamut, and quite a few in the middle too. If this is true, it begs the obvious question. Why would you keep any of the negative relationships at all? What's to gain by allowing a draining and destructive relationship to take up any space in your life? Your precious emotional resources are not limitless, so why give them away only to regret it time and time again? Is this done out of pity? Guilt? Obligation? A desire not to hurt someone's feelings? Maybe it's something more self-serving? Perhaps an awareness that even if certain friends aren't a healthy friendship choice, you love them and would miss them terribly if they weren't around. Do you have fun with them but know the fun includes activities you shouldn't be engaging in? Are you in a dating or love relationship and dread potential feelings of jealousy and hurt which might surface should you break up, so you hang on and go through the same damaging cycles to avoid dealing with the feelings? Sound familiar? These are extremely powerful inhibitors that can keep you yoked to a friendship or relationship that you would otherwise be smart to avoid.

We've each been down this road and can tell you from personal experience that you must own the decision and deal with it head on. Make a resolution to set healthy boundaries! Just because someone has been part of your life for years doesn't mean you're obligated to keep them in your life now; things change. A friend may have helped you out in the past, but he or she doesn't have the right to make you miserable in the present. Remove the negative. Your party buddy is no buddy at all if that relationship influences you to make poor choices; reroute your interests. Knowing you'll have to deal with the pangs of hurt and jealousy when breaking up with your boyfriend/girlfriend is no reason to give up the rest of your life and live with regret. Don't run from critical decisions.

We sometimes over-analyze and torment ourselves with decisions that need to be made. We're scared to make a mistake that may cost us our happiness and bring regret, but on the flipside, we can't afford to be wrong and stay in an unhealthy, unhappy relationship. No doubt this can be horribly confusing, but ask God to enter in and listen to him. If you're open, you'll find he's very straightforward. It's simply up to you to seek his word and embrace what he's saying. It's all there for the asking:

"But seek first his kingdom and his righteousness, and
all these things will be given to you as well."

(Mt. 6:33)

Remember, with all decluttering, the basic premise is to remove the bad so you have time and energy to devote to the good. Ditch the drain! It's your responsibility to decide who to keep and who to cut loose and, once you do, put the wheels in motion to back up your choice.

Cut 'Em Loose

Before we continue, we have a point to clarify. When we talk about cutting someone loose, we aren't referring to a friend who's having a bad day and is grumpy, or even someone that's going through a rough patch in their lives and is difficult to be around. Perhaps they're exhausting you a bit because they legitimately need your help. We aren't giving you a get out of jail free card to break up with your boy/girlfriend whom has a reasonable request or concern. Even right relationships will have wrong moments or seasons that are worth working through. We're talking about relationships with people who continually leave you feeling worse than before you saw or spoke to them, or those who negatively impact you and cause you to stumble and stray. There are individuals who think nothing of tapping into your resources, but don't do anything constructive with the assistance and are back for more time and time again.

The idea here is not to ditch healthy and positive relationships because you're feeling lazy or stubborn, and not to keep bad ones out of sheer obligation or pity. The only obligation you should feel is in honestly acknowledging the situation and being responsible in doing your part.

Hand Up vs. Handout

For the record, it's not being heartless to acknowledge there's a tremendous difference between a hand up and a handout. It might sound like a cliché, but there's so much truth packed in this concept. There are many times when a hand up is genuinely warranted and we encourage a loving response; reach out and get involved. Be wise in your assessment of each situation, though, so you can recognize when nothing more than a handout is being sought. This is no small task, and sometimes you may feel tormented by your emotions. There will be times you desperately want to help but know if you do, you're really doing your friend a disservice—disabling them instead of enabling them. *Tough love*. Think about how God handles us when we need help. He doesn't pave the way on easy street or do the work for us; at least that hasn't been our experience! Go to God with your concerns. He's a wise and experienced counselor on the subject and will not only guide you in your decisions, but shore you up after you've made the right ones!

Sorting It Out

[*Sherry*] I have developed an internal category method I utilize when evaluating friendships and relationships. In explaining this method, I run the risk of seriously offending some people, but it's pertinent to the topic and a leap of faith I must take if I am to be true to our discussion. (Insert me wincing here!)

My category method is a fundamentally basic concept, but the implementation is what renders it so helpful. The system is designed to make me more aware of the need for thoughtful, intentional choices. My mom always told me we become responsible for that which we know. After reading this, you'll have a fresh and keen awareness and will no longer be able to claim ignorance. Our prayer is this insight motivates you to make beneficial relationship changes.

Suppose you have eight categories of friends, ranging from the acquaintance you make small talk with when dropping your kids off at school (1), all the way up to the best of your best friends (8). Determine the starting category for each friend in your current circle.

You may have a friend you love dearly but talking to him or her more than once a month, which you continue to do, is irritating and unpleasant. You may call that person a category 5 friend (but you know the rating should really be only a 2 or 3).

Category 8, as suggested, is reserved for your very best friend. The person you feel safe telling everything to. The friend who loves you unconditionally, is always there if and when you need help, and provides loving, wise counsel. That friend has earned that place and it's a fitting spot.

How about the person in category 2 that you wish you could spend more time with, but you haven't made the effort to carve out opportunities to do so? You genuinely enjoy being around this person and the feeling is mutual. Perhaps that person should really be a 6 or a 7? It's just as crucial to make time for the important people as it is to free yourself up from the ones that are not. Consider your category 3 friend that you dislike being around but do it for the sake of a particular situation. While it doesn't seem you waste *too* much time with them, they're only a 3 but they're still taking up space and energy. If you eliminate that person altogether, you'll free up more space to move your friend who is a 2 to a 6. Harsh but true. It's cumulative and it all counts.

Your Personal Touch

You need to make up your own unique categories and determine what defines each of them. Take a hard look at what you have. Does it work for you? If not, you're certainly not alone. Most people have some rearranging to do. As you might imagine, this is where it can get a bit tricky, awkward, and sometimes downright difficult, but we promise you it'll be worth it in the long run. As my husband says, "It isn't that life is too short; it's that life is too long to live with unhappiness or regret." There's so much logic in that sentiment.

Does the thought of rearranging bring out feelings of guilt? That may not be such a bad thing—if it's the right kind of guilt. Good guilt motivates. Let's say you feel regret that you've been shortchanging yourself by spending time with people you'd rather not be around, and consequently not having enough time for the people you want to be around. This guilt is beneficial if you use it to make positive changes. After you implement change, however, you must let the guilt go. At that point the guilt's job is done and nothing good can come of hanging onto it. On the other hand, if you're burdened with bad guilt because you feel sorry for the people that you're moving down in category or removing altogether, stop! Obviously, do your best to be kind and compassionate, but remind yourself that it's healthy and necessary to take care of your own heart first. Even though it may not seem so initially, it really is a win-win for both you and your friends.

Consider how the category method allows you to tap into and enjoy what you treasure most in each friend, and in return, this sets your friend up for success. Think about it from their perspective. If you were in their shoes, would you want someone to spend time with you out of pity or obligation? We would hope not! There's a good possibility they sense your frustration with them; no one wants to feel they are a constant disappointment. Perhaps they feel they've always fallen short in your eyes or are under pressure to behave a certain way for you and this burdens them? Most of the time, you'll find that if you're unhappy with your friend for one reason or the other, there's a pretty good chance they're not terribly thrilled with you either. Do both of you a favor and set honest boundaries that come from your heart.

Recently, while dealing with an unhealthy relationship, Ryan decided to remove an individual almost entirely from his sphere of influence. Basically he moved a 4 or 5 category person to a 1. Ryan is the most kindhearted, caring, understanding guy in the world. We know much thought and prayer went into his decision and when the change was made, Ryan's reaction was, "I am so glad it's finally over; the mess is gone." The mess gone? We were a little surprised to hear such a sentiment come from him, but it drove the point home that there's a time and place when change is necessary for everyone.

When you are re-categorizing, some relational shifts will be subtle and hardly noticeable, but others may require just pulling the rug out and making swift adjustments. Either way, if a change is in order, we encourage you to be brave and make it happen. If this makes you nervous or uncomfortable, take baby steps at first. Start with a move that's minor in nature, learn from the experience, and build upon it.

Unavoidable Pitfalls

Unfortunately, though, the truth is no matter how tactfully or lovingly you implement downward category shifts, we're sure you can see the potential problems. What if you move your category 6 friend down to 3? The weekly chats turn into a monthly chat and your friend is one unhappy camper? If you feel comfortable enough, talk to your friend before they are affected by the changes and explain what has prompted your feelings. We wouldn't necessarily advise you to talk "category method" or share with them the reduced number you've relegated them to, but speak from the heart with compassion. If you choose not to address it on the front side and your friend confronts you, speak honestly. You don't have to be mean and hurtful to get a point across.

Will there be awkward moments? Hmmmm... probably! But think about it. Is passing on those awkward moments worth all the time wasted and spent being somewhere you don't want to be with someone you dread being with? For us, we'd take awkward any day! And again, your friend, even if hurt, would most likely appreciate your honesty. Yes, you might lose a "friend" or two along the way. Or they may lose you. When you move a 6 down to a 2, they may make YOU a zero! Unfortunately, that's a chance you must be willing to take, but even that's better than wasting your time and constantly suffering the fallout from an unhealthy relationship. Just as with natural resources, which become depleted over time, our time and energy can get exhausted as well. Why on earth would you exhaust your resources for something that offers you a negative return? Spend it wisely since we don't get any of it back!

Lesser of the Evils

All of this may initially come across a bit calculated and insensitive, but if you work through the process as its intended, we believe you'll find the opposite to be true. When the logistics of relationship decluttering are presented in a black and white perspective, the abstract components become more tangible and easier to grasp. Real life is not cut and dry, and it's inviting to hide behind that ambiguity, get confused with emotion, and procrastinate indefinitely. You'll never realize what you're missing if you deny, disregard, or don't even know the truth. The category method requires an honest assessment of your feelings and considerate, deliberate actions—a winning one-two punch.

Yes, some decisions will be crazy hard and you may feel anguish like never before, but we're not advocating you work through this as an emotionless robot. Quite the contrary. We hope you will be able to see your situation clearly, and we pray you can gently and lovingly implement what you believe needs to be done. We aren't suggesting being harsh or hurtful in your approach, but we unequivocally believe God calls his people to stand up and do the right thing, even when unpopular or difficult. There may be hurt feelings, anger, and grieving on both sides of the relationship. If the going gets too tough, allow yourself the room to gradually work through it. Just don't be deterred! Reflect on the fact that you are choosing the lesser of the evils; this is precisely where the black and white of it all can keep you on track.

Pre-emptive Planning

Downward shifts can be painful, even when you're the one initiating it. Perhaps you've come to the conclusion that it's time to end your dating or love relationship. In this case, you're not dealing with just a category shift but a person removal. Going into this, you might fear the painful time that's coming. Guys, no eye rolling here! We know you have feelings too. You anticipate the lump in your throat, the sick feeling in your stomach, the tears that will be shed, and the sleepless nights on the horizon. Talk about anxiety! Be proactive and put things in place to help you through it. Share what you're going through with close and trusted friends, and seek their support, encouragement, and company. Plan activities that will keep you busy and get caught up on your long standing to-do's so you feel a sense of purpose and accomplishment. Perhaps sign up for a class you've been thinking about taking or devote some extra time to your favorite hobby. Is there a friend or relative you've been meaning to visit? Perfect time! Busying yourself with healthy activities is not denial or running away. You've made a difficult decision, and it's smart to spend a bit of extra time caring for yourself while you recover. You can't remove all the pain and fill the gap entirely, which is actually good. This time is when you gather an abundance of lessons on love and life and, through them, you're empowered to make better future choices for yourself, as well as mentor others down the road. With some effort, you can ease the transition and brush your knees off a bit more quickly.

Put on the Armor of God

As Christians, we often feel we're expected to perform a certain way. While being Christian insinuates a high standard of behavior, God didn't intend for us to replicate doormats or punching bags. Are you familiar with the phrase "Armor of God"? There are a string of verses that compile God's directive on defending against evil. Through them, God equips us with the armor needed to carry this out. We are to suit up with the belt of truth, the breastplate of righteousness, the shield of faith, the helmet of salvation, and the sword of the Spirit. Take the time to read Ephesians 6:10-18 in its entirety, but even with just the bits we've provided here, God's instruction is abundantly clear. We're not called to lie down and succumb to abuse, temptation, and evil; we are to stand tall and strong. Yes, there are great expectations on our lives, but they should never be at the expense of our morals and values.

Along life's journey, there will be people you're delighted to embrace as friends, some you feel called to help, and others you're better off keeping at arm's length. For the latter, you can still pray for the person or point them in the right direction, but you don't necessarily need to be the point man. God may have someone else better suited for the task lined up just down the road. This isn't permission to shirk responsibility when it should be yours, rather an argument for the position that we aren't called to be everything to everybody. Sometimes stepping back or passing is the best choice and the decision God would prefer you make as well.

Something else to bear in mind. It's not your duty to save everyone. In fact, remember, you don't personally save anyone anyway. While you may just be trying to lend assistance, know your place. Remember what Jesus said: "I am the way and the truth and the life. No one comes to the Father except through me" (John 14:6). Jesus went after sinners and outcasts with the purpose of getting them cleaned up and saved. He didn't, however, help everyone, because not everyone was open to what he offered. Take the Sadducees and the Pharisees for instance. Their religious stance was such that they were closed off to the Holy Spirit. There are those who are "open" to being helped and those who aren't. Use thoughtful discernment when deciding where your responsibility starts and stops and what resources you are called to expend.

Are you a Lead-er?

There are always lead-ees and lead-ers. Which are you? Can you disseminate the difference? When my [*Sherry's*] boys were in high school, we had many discussions regarding this concept. Occasionally, one of the boys would argue that they should be allowed to spend time with someone or be somewhere that I might not wholeheartedly approve of. Their contention was for Christians to penetrate the lives of unbelievers, they may need to spend some time on the unbelievers' turf. Your first thought might be that I'm completely naïve if I didn't see right through them, that Ryan and Devin were crafty and simply finagling a way to get permission for the Saturday night party. If you knew them, however, you would understand nothing is further from the truth. There's solid rationale to their argument and I agree we shouldn't live in bubbles and wall ourselves off from people who believe or act differently. That would go against the very nature of evangelical living. The key question is, are you strong enough to be a lead-er, or do you run the risk of being led?

Think about that for a moment. Attending a kegger is not the wisest choice for a recovering alcoholic, even if that person's sole intention is being present to impact people for Christ. Leave that mission for someone else who has no temptation in that arena. You know your weaknesses and it's prudent to remain diligent and guarded. Remove obvious opportunities for Satan to trip you up. He would love nothing more than to watch you fall. You won't be any good to yourself or anyone else if you succumb to the temptations of the problem or environment you intend to stand against. What message would that send? Ouch!

That being said, often those best equipped to speak on an issue have walked through, survived, and thrived beyond it. It would be a shame not to benefit others with the wisdom of those experiences, but what a conundrum that poses. Bear the lead-er vs. lead-ee question in mind, put safeguards in place, and set both yourself and the recipient of your good works up for the best chance of success.

Obviously, we're not advocating you put yourself in a detrimental or dangerous situation, although, taking a calculated risk is sometimes necessary. For instance, if Christian missionaries never visited less stable parts of the world, how many countries would have little or no teaching on Christ? First and foremost, seek God's will in all you do.

We wish we could provide hard and fast rules for the "To-do's" and "To-don'ts," but there are as many different scenarios as there are people in commune with God. He made each of us unique and the call on our lives just as distinct. The Bible offers guidelines for everyone, but it's your relationship with Christ that directs your individual life application. There may be times when it's beneficial for God's Kingdom that you step outside your comfort zone and into an unfamiliar setting, even into a situation that doesn't offer security. There will also be times when it isn't. Just be absolutely certain in either case that you're where God is calling you to be.

Make a Social Statement

Another aspect of relationship decluttering involves 21st century communication. Email and social networking sites can consume massive quantities of your time. Are they really worth the return for the time spent? It often seems with this communication, quality is traded for quantity. Sure, we'll send a quick text or email to a friend to let them know we're thinking of them, but we hesitate time and time again to pick up the phone and actually speak to them. Lindon is better at still picking up the phone than Sherry, but we'll both admit that we enjoy the convenience and perks that texting affords. We've learned, however, this comes at a price. Not only do we have yet another area to declutter, all of the text messages, but there's also no replacement for personal touch or human communication. True intentions can get lost in translation and cause far more harm than good. Take the time to call. Call to ask how your friends are, to find out what's new in their lives, and to see if there's anything they need. Sometimes detecting emotions and truth is far easier with a live voice; it's harder to hide behind. Don't pass on caring for those you truly love in order to keep in touch with hundreds of people who don't matter all that much.

[*Sherry*] How many of you receive and delete multiple forwarded emails? I finally had enough. I was wasting more time deleting than I was reading and responding to important items. I finally emailed all of my friends and asked them kindly to refrain from including me in their email distribution list. I explained that while I welcomed an individual note or message, I didn't spend much time on my home computer these days and honestly didn't have time for anything not of a personal nature. As far as I know, I didn't offend anyone, and I even got a few emails back applauding my "bold" (I had to laugh!) move and suggesting they might do the same.

And hold on to your hats because this is an earth shattering admission. I have been seriously contemplating canceling my page on a popular networking site. One of our kids was tired of the drama and, in a heroic move, canceled that account. No small task for a very connected 20-something-year-old. I was so impressed and moved by this, I just may follow suit. Lindon would wholeheartedly support this as he calls it "Fakebook" anyway! He's not fond of social networking for personal communication and feels it's a breeding ground for destructive and invasive behavior. Yes, it's fun to share information and easy to do it en masse, but we often completely overlook the compromising position we put ourselves in when sharing intimate and sensitive information. Every detail of our lives becomes public knowledge and, in the wrong hands, this could be disastrous. If you utilize social networking sites for personal use, be responsible, careful, and conservative in what you share. The truth is the friends I really care about, and want to stay in touch with, will be the people I take the time to personally speak to and see anyway.

While I share Lindon's concerns, these sites have their uses. For instance, they can be invaluable when it comes to finding old classmates for an upcoming reunion. They have also made a significant impact on today's marketing world; we can't wait to have a *Declutter Now!* page. Social networking is a great tool for businesses and ministries to utilize, reaching thousands of people, often with little or no cost.

There is one last underlying concern to mention, a common thread that runs throughout the modes of modern communication. When people hide behind the mask of texting, emails, social networking sites, instant messaging, etc., they often act in a way far different than they normally would in face-to-face contact. There is less accountability, more boldness, and a feeling of freedom to say something they would've never dreamed of if they'd been engaging in a personal interaction. If not managed with extreme care and caution, this freedom can be destructive.

Appearances can be Deceiving

You may be thinking at this point that we're against the advancement of technology and have turned into some of the grumpy senior citizens you know who appreciate the ways gone by and don't understand all this new-fangled stuff. Not true! There's a time and place for reaping the benefits of modern innovations, and we indulge as much as the next person. If these same innovations are abused, however, and quality and personal touch are removed, we lose in the long run. Make an effort to preserve the important relational aspects of your friendships. Avoid cluttering your life with things that have the appearance of streamlining when, in hindsight, they will just add more problems and clutter, and fewer moments of genuine joy.

A Word to the Men

[*Lindon*] Just as important as what you're doing with your time and with whom you're spending it, is where you're spending it. I feel compelled to offer a disclaimer. I'm well aware that much of what will be presented in this section isn't reserved exclusively for men, but I firmly believe God specifically calls men to emotionally, physically, financially, and spiritually lead their families. We have a duty, and we must take this seriously and behave with honor and integrity. Men, it's our job to protect and preserve the sanctity of our marriage and we must be cognizant that every single action and decision we make will either positively or negatively impact it. The significance and truth of this point cannot be overstated. Would you rather benefit or detract from the wellbeing of your marriage and family?

Men, it can be something as simple as the Friday night hangout at the local bar or perhaps, somewhere even more edgy, but you must consider how spending your time in these establishments can really throw your moral compass off, not to mention other things! Is it okay to meet your friend for a beer every once in a while? Personally, I say sure, but truthfully, I would rather see you go home and enjoy that beer with your wife—even if she doesn't drink.

Some may argue that bars and the like don't make decisions for the man; that it's up to him to make the right decisions because no matter where he may go, he'll be faced with choices. While there is truth to this, the fact remains that when you're in an establishment that's geared for alcohol consumption and the single crowd, you're tempting fate and setting yourself up for the possibility of disaster.

And if the moral part of this argument isn't speaking to you yet, think about the practical side: your time and wallet. There are men who spend hundreds of dollars at the bars every Friday and Saturday. They live from paycheck to paycheck and are truly working for the weekend, but for all the wrong reasons. I can think of a dozen ways I'd rather be spending my time and money, couldn't you? Wouldn't you rather take your wife out, treat your kids to a ball game, or do something special that would be worthy of creating a memory (or a memory card)? If you like to fish, make it a point to plan trips where the whole family can go. Real life can be exciting enough; it doesn't require a night on the town with your guy friends to create excitement!

Guard Yourselves

You've all heard the stories about the guy no one would have ever suspected of cheating on his wife, exposed for living a double life. He may even have multiple wives or children conceived out of wedlock. This isn't just in the news, but is happening in your neighborhood, local community, and even in your church. The internet provides an effortless conduit for inappropriate behavior. The attraction and addiction to pornography today is in epic proportions. Guard yourselves men (and women)! Stay as far away from anything that remotely resembles temptation and trouble as you can!

Sherry and I have an agreement that whenever possible, we won't go out with friends of the opposite gender, whether it be for lunch, a drink or the like, unless we go together. That may sound rigid and non-trusting but just the opposite is true. To keep what we hold sacred protected, we've set up guidelines and boundaries. Sherry and I are true blue to each other and would *never*, and I mean *NEVER*, stray in any way that would put our marriage at risk, so there's simply no reason to put ourselves in a position that might jeopardize our intentions. There's *no* meeting, *no* drink, *no* event that's more important than our marriage. Period! We need to avoid even the appearance of evil.

I am reminded of Billy Graham. He never allowed himself to be alone with a woman other than his wife, under any circumstance, and would even refuse to step into an elevator if there was a woman in there alone. People are always watching and not everyone has your best interests at heart, so you'd be wise to eliminate any potential problems beforehand to avoid bigger problems later. Your reputation is everything!

I'm also a firm believer that men have got to put on their blinders and keep them on. Think about the horse that wears blinders to stay focused on the race. Men, you *must* keep your eyes straight ahead and your focus on whatever your race is. Why look around for trouble if you can avoid it instead? Wandering eyes lead to a wandering heart and temptations that can be too powerful to overcome. Don't allow room for any temptation in your life; none.

Realizing Responsibility

Men are called to guide, direct, and protect their homes with a loving heart and caring spirit. We are not called to lord over our families but rather to lead by example. I'm not sure many men could, in good conscience, justify their current behavior if they truthfully reflected on their performance as a husband and father.

What about your responsibility as a friend? Are you encouraging others to join you in places that I'm suggesting you shouldn't even be in to begin with? What reflection is this on you as a friend? Not a good one!

I must reiterate that I realize I've singled out and specifically picked on the guys here, but with good reason. God charges men to be the stronger vessel and stand on the side of what's right, no matter what. If you're married, then you are the guardian of the family; it falls on your shoulders to make wise decisions for the good of the family as a whole. I've got a huge heart for ministering to men and it grieves me to hear the directives given to them diluted or ignored—the polar opposite of what should be happening.

This being said, women can certainly heed my advice and apply it to their lives as well. Women can also make poor choices, compromise their marriage and families, and fall short of what God intended for them. We've all heard about the married gal who appeared to be the perfect homemaker, exposed as a modern day "cougar," running around with a boy-toy half her age. No one is exempt from temptation and bad decisions.

Freedom within Boundaries

I believe that boundaries create freedom. *What?* That makes no sense at all, Lindon! Ahhhhh, but it really does. Allow me to explain. You can have fun, be creative, and enjoy your life to the fullest with no regrets when you operate within healthy boundaries. You only find yourself in trouble when you veer from the moral and just path for your life. It may seem like a good idea at the time, but it will invariably end up detrimental to your wellbeing. Becoming a slave to lies, walking around with a heavy, guilt-filled heart, and losing all that you have is no freedom at all. Yes, the connotation of "boundaries" might elicit a negative reaction at first, but consider the consequences of life outside them and you'll quickly discover the opposite is true. Boundaries actually prevent you from being plagued with heartache, shame, and regret, and this in turn breeds true freedom indeed.

Here is an analogy that may help put this into better perspective—the horse and the hotwire. I trained horses for twenty-three years. Many horse owners use a hot wire system as an effective means to keep their horses corralled. When you have a horse that constantly pushes on the fence to test for weak rails (the grass is always greener on the other side, of course!), he's instantly reminded he must stay on his side of the fence. A sudden jolt of high-voltage electricity lets the horse know just where the boundaries are. Now, within their fence, they can run, jump, buck, play, and have the time of their lives, all while staying under the protection of their owner. Once they leave the boundary of the fence and the protection it provides, they're completely on their own.

It's kind of like that for us. If we keep testing the boundaries, instead of living within them, we're going to get shocked. If we continue to press and eventually end up on the other side of the fence, we'll be left to our own devices without God's covering on our lives. At that point, we're nothing more than bait for all the ills of the world and for Satan, who aggressively seeks out those who are vulnerable and living unprotected. The reality of life is it's never greener on the other side of the fence; not by a longshot. God will make sure we have all we need on the right side of the fence; our job is to stay there and appreciate it to the fullest.

Live, laugh, and love, but do it in a way that makes God proud and leaves you guilt free. When you get to the point where you live fully and freely within healthy boundaries, it's then that you'll find true contentment and joy.

Jesus tells us in Matthew 11:28-30: "Come to me, all you who are weary and burdened, and I will give you rest. Take my yoke upon you and learn from me, for I am gentle and humble in heart, and you will find rest for your souls. For my yoke is easy and my burden is light."

Living a life with Jesus means the responsibilities are being shared; shared with someone who has far more power and ability than we do. Jesus allows us to make our own choices, but he hopes we'll choose to live within his protective covering. If there's so much to gain by living this way—and even more to lose by not—doesn't it make sense to stay within the safety that's offered? Think about the sacrifice Jesus made to provide this safety to us, and then consider the little that he's asking in return. It hardly seems fair that all we're asked to do is live an honorable life filled with the joy of the Spirit.

Man up, Soldier

So, is an occasional drink with your buddy or a weekend fishing trip with the guys okay? My short answer is, sure! There are definitely benefits to time spent this way; just make sure it doesn't become your priority. Be certain you don't clutter your life with so many of these types of activities that you squeeze out time reserved for nurturing the most important relationships: those with God, your wife, and your family.

You might be reading this and thinking it's garbage; just something to take away your fun and make you live a boring life with constrictive rules. You're building a wall to keep what I am saying out, but believe me when I tell you the only wall you should build is the one that keeps temptation and evil out, while containing and protecting the treasures you hold dear in your family, friends, and relationships. Man up, soldier, and join the program! There's life-changing truth here, and I pray you'll grab it and hold on tight.

Recognizing the Many Faces of Clutter

Decluttering your relationships proves that clutter can enter your life in so many unsuspecting ways. You know that sinking feeling when you've just committed to something you wish you didn't? That's *regretful clutter*. How about when your insides are grumbling because you're spending time with someone and itching to be elsewhere? That's *frustration clutter*.

The guilt that weighs you down and causes you to make decisions out of duty is *obligation clutter*. The doormat feeling when you allow someone to take advantage of you is *victim clutter*. And the remorseful feeling you have when you succumb to temptation you knew better about is *shameful clutter*. Recognize these scenarios in advance, before they play out, so you'll be able to make good decisions on the front side and have less clutter and clean up on the back.

Healthy Heart Livin'

By now you're beginning to understand how decluttering relationships can positively impact your entire life and why clear, healthy boundaries are necessary to accomplish this. This need not be a robotic approach, simply an intentional one. How freeing would it be to never again respond with a yes out of obligation when every cell in your body is screaming NO? How liberating would it be to know that you're not wasting time out of fear, guilt, or pity, yet truly enjoying your time with those who matter most to your heart? How warming would it be to see the positive changes you make in your life bearing a wonderful witness to a friend, who in turn may find their own freedom and joy in decluttering? How freeing would it be to live guilt and regret free while enjoying all the treasures God intended for you? How much more useful could you be to God if you were where God wanted you to be and with those he desires you with? It may be your Christian circle where you're surrounded by those who lift you up and encourage you, or it may be helping and witnessing to a lost soul in a foreign country. Whatever the case, the point is to discern God's voice in all of your choices so the end result is effective, worthwhile, and positive.

"And we know that in all things God works for the good of those who love him, who have been called according to his purpose" (Rom. 8:28). God has so much in store for you; he just needs your availability to receive all that he wants to bless you with.

Be realistic in your endeavor. Imperfect people can't create perfect relationships no matter how hard they try, so scrap that expectation. Rather, gauge your success by what you do with what you have. Ask yourself:

Are you willing to remove yourself from harmful and hurtful relationships so you can invest more time and energy in people who are deserving of your love and attention?

Are you prepared to give up the distractions in your life, even if you enjoy them, because they are detracting from your family time and depleting your resources?

Are you equipped with the armor of God to do the works he is calling you to do?

To each of these questions, we pray your answer is yes! Get started and soon you'll find yourself with less clutter in your heart and life and the ability to truly enjoy the life that God has so lovingly prepared for you. Live intentionally, make courageous decisions, and remain steadfast in your decluttering journey.

Chapter 3

Divorcing Debt and Marrying Financial Freedom

DIVORCE GENERALLY HAS THE CONNOTATION of a dirty word but not so much when it refers to something you truly *should* separate yourself from. Divorcing debt definitely qualifies as a divorce you can feel great about! We want to empower you with a healthy approach to managing your finances and we'd love to see you toss your debt into the declutter bin forever, make wise financial decisions from this point forward, and be married to a lifestyle you can be proud of.

The news media is ripe with statistics on consumer debt. From mortgages and auto loans to credit cards to home equity and student loans, Americans are up to their eyeballs in debt. For some it's a slow buildup and for others a rapid ascent to the top—or bottom actually. Like the older gentleman who one day realized his belt buckle was hiding far under his belly, the result of many years of good eating, we have become fat with debt. Akin to a good diet and workout plan, it's going to take some legitimate effort, along with dedication, to shave inches off your debt and lower the balances of your financial scales. As with exercise, simply thinking about it isn't going to get you into the shape you desire. Luckily, we've got each other, so get ready for that first step and together we'll walk through making some simple, yet profoundly impactful, changes in your financial health. Once started, you'll feel so encouraged about what you've begun that continuing on your journey will be easier than expected.

Admittedly, we're not financial "experts," but we are experts at real life and come to you chock full of experience and lessons learned. Lindon has worked in the banking industry for over ten years and ran a business of his own for almost two decades. For over sixteen years, Sherry has been a full charge bookkeeper / office manager for a company and has been instrumental in making financial business decisions for them. In addition, Sherry managed her household for years as a single parent with a single income. Although these are just a sampling of the experiences which have equipped us, they alone bring a lifetime of well-rounded knowledge to the table. We've lived, worked, struggled, borrowed, and paid the price. Fortunately, we gained a boatload of wisdom along the way too. This chapter includes strategies, ideas, and tips to declutter the financial chaos you might be living with. Even if you're in pretty good shape, let's make what you have work harder and smarter for you. It's not just about making more money, but often about doing more with what you have. Ultimately, we would like to see you do more with less!

Our advice is real-world and practical. We've no intention of throwing fancy terms at you or sharing complicated, strategic investment strategies. We'll leave that to the financial gurus. What we'll provide, however, is advice that we've found invaluable in our attempt to get to the altar of financial freedom.

You may be aware of an underlying theme brewing in the decluttering concept thus far, one that you'll notice even more clearly as you continue to read and tie all the topics together. FREEDOM! Freedom from what's less important so you have more of what is. Our motivation was prompted by an overwhelming urge to increase our service to the Lord in a mighty way. We weren't exactly sure what that looked like but knew an overall decluttering was required for us to have the time, energy, and finances at our disposal to figure it out. We had to ready ourselves, and decluttering our finances was, and still is, a critical part of the cumulative process.

Here are a couple of our favorite verses which speak directly to this subject:

"Whoever loves money never has money enough; whoever loves wealth is never satisfied with his income. This too is meaningless."
                                                                (Eccl. 5:10)

Solomon knew those who seek money would never find the happiness they falsely believed it would provide. Have you found this to be true? Can money really buy true contentment? We believe genuine, everlasting contentment only comes from God, and no matter how many dollars you put together, money is no match or substitute for Christ.

"Keep your lives free from the love of money and be content with what you have, because God has said, 'Never will I leave you; never will I forsake you.'"
                                                                (Heb. 13:5)

He's there for the long haul, folks, and we need to keep our eyes on him.

The crux of this chapter involves revamping your thinking about what's truly important and making the changes required to pursue them instead of chasing the almighty dollar. It's critical for married couples to see eye to eye and have common goals. If only one spouse sees a need or problem in the financial spectrum, as a team, you will never realize a successful end result.

And while you both need to be on the same page, you'll each have different contributions to make. Men should have cash in their pockets, not debit cards. And women, know this, gone are your days of cash back with purchases to mask your extra spending. Awkward pause? Okay, surely we jest . These bad habits aren't limited to only one gender or the other, but the logical conclusion is that bad habits must change for both if you want a different end result in the equation.

Track the Spending Trail

The first order of action will be tracking everything you buy for one week, and we mean *everything*. Every pack of gum, every latte purchase, every quick lunch from the ninety-nine cent menu at the local drive-thru. It ALL counts. Don't include household bills such as utilities, auto loans, mortgage payments, weekly grocery shopping trips, etc. This list is intended for what you spend on any incidentals which wouldn't be considered monthly budget expenses. It'll represent all of your cash out-of-pocket spending, including debit purchases and, heaven forbid, the should-be-off-limits credit card for personal use.

Before you begin, take a stab at how much you believe your total weekly spending amount will be. Jot that number down and tuck it away so you can later compare your projection to what was actually spent. There are very few things we're willing to bet on, but we're prepared to wager you're going to be dumbfounded at how quickly the dollars add up and how much more you spent than anticipated. The first time I [*Sherry*] tracked personal spending, I was completely blown away. This exercise alone forever curtailed my spending habits. In seven short days I became far more conscious of how much money I was actually spending and acutely aware of the difference between what I truly needed versus what I merely wanted or thought I needed. In all its simplicity, this exercise provided an eye-opening snapshot of my true spending habits. (As a side note, this exercise is also highly effective before attempting to change your eating habits. Writing down everything you put into your mouth for one week will equip you with the data you need to formulate a successful plan of attack. Trust us!) Can you relate to times in your life when making a change felt like a grueling, painstaking effort every step of the way? Well, hang on for at least one easy transition. After just a week of logging spending habits, the change will seem almost effortless. Your new awareness will naturally affect your thoughts, actions, and even desires. Sound too good to be true? Give it a try; we suspect you'll be pleasantly surprised.

To track effectively, keep a paper and pen with you at all times. Collect receipts along the way and log every dime you spend. At the end of the week, add up all you've spent. Log your purchases into categories to highlight where you tend to part with your hard-earned dollars most. The patterns you uncover will be instrumental in your effort to streamline and cut out waste.

Next, take what you've learned from your tracking exercise and declutter the unnecessary. Of course it's okay to leave yourself a few bucks for an occasional treat, but for the most part, revamp your habits and make your spending count.

The "B" Word

After you have a handle on your necessary versus frivolous personal spending, it's time to put together your monthly budget. Yes, we said it—the "B" word! Many people have an immediate visceral reaction to the thought of budgeting and, if this is how you feel, try and set aside all preconceived notions or negative feelings you may have. We understand the idea of having to discipline yourself with your finances, make sacrifices, or face ugly realities are deterrents for embracing a budget, but the alternative is a life of financial bondage and heartache. By far, this is the lesser of the two evils. What we're presenting is a practical, realistic, uncomplicated relationship with your money which will create a new, positive foundation. The budgeting template we'll share may seem simplistic in nature, but don't discount simplicity. There's a lifetime of helpful experience and wisdom in what we impart to you, basic or not.

We're old school in some senses, and we still write our monthly budget on an 8 x 11 sheet of paper. Sherry likes to have it with her at all times. With all the technology available, many of you might prefer utilizing more advanced means with which to create your budget such as spreadsheets, home accounting programs, or PDA's. Go for it! The concepts are the same regardless of which method you use.

To begin, make a comprehensive list of every monthly expense and bill you currently have, the dollar amount, and if applicable, its due date. Also include line items you should be saving money for each month such as auto and medical expenses. Here's an example to get you started:

Mortgage - 1st - $1750
Electric bill - 26th - $260
Water bill - 6th - $140
Cellular bill – 22nd - $175
Credit Card #1 - 15th - $150 (hopefully this isn't even on your list)
Credit Card #2 - 22nd - $75 (same goes for this one too)
Tithe - $
People Fund - $
Auto insurance – 19th - $184
Her spending - $240
His spending - $120 (yup, he gets less—HA!)
Her gas - $100
His gas - $240 (and THIS is why!)
Groceries - $400
Haircuts - $50
Nails - $80 (everyone deserves a small luxury, IF you can afford it)
Doctor / Rx fund - $80
House maintenance fund - $76
Auto fund - $75 (this should be for maintenance, registration, etc.)
Pool maintenance fund - $25
Christmas fund - $80
Birthday / Special occasion fund - $50
Date Nights - $100
Savings - $200

While our list may not be representative of your unique obligations and lifestyle, it'll give you an idea how it should look. You'll notice each of us has a line item for spending. We strongly promote the pay-yourself-first theory. Within the scope of your financial situation, you must determine how much you will pay yourself for personal spending: the items you spent on during your tracking exercise. Remember we asked you to declutter the unnecessary but still leave yourself extra for a little something? If you don't enjoy some of the fruits of your labor, even to a minimal degree, you'll lose heart. Your financial position may be such that your fun money is extremely limited, but as available and as sensible, take care of you first. For men, note that your Saturday golf outing or fishing trip shouldn't come out of the monthly budget, but from what you've been able to save up from your own spending money. And ladies, same goes for you. Your coffee or luncheon dates should also come from your individual spending fund. There's something to be said for hunkering down and being disciplined.

The next step is to list all of your pay periods for the month. If you're married, combine both net paychecks. For instance, Sherry gets paid every Friday, but Lindon only gets paid every other week. This results in two Fridays using only Sherry's income, and combined income amounts for the other two Fridays.

Now comes the challenging part. Keeping the due dates in mind, take each line item you've listed and determine the best pay period in which to list the expense. If you have more bills due at a particular time of the month than another, list some earlier in the month than they are actually due so your weekly requirements are spread evenly throughout the month. If you have a larger expense, such as your mortgage or rent payment, you may need to allot money from more than just one pay period. Weekly expenses such as personal spending, groceries, gas, etc., should be divided up evenly up over each pay period. Think of putting pieces of a jigsaw puzzle together where they belong. You are strategically plotting the best place for each piece of your budget to go.

See the mock budget below, which assumes every Friday is payday, for an idea on how to create your first draft. Don't be disappointed if it takes a few tries, at least, to achieve a successfully balanced working budget. Finagling and rearranging is par for the course and, depending on the complexity of your finances, you may have to write and revise, and then rewrite again. Once you've established a template, though, the subsequent months will be easier; just remember to update as needed.

APRIL

7th

$100 - Groceries
$30 - His spending
$60 - Her spending
$60 - His gas
$25 - Her gas
$150 - Credit Card #1 (4/15)
$500 - Tithe - %
$100 - Date Nights
$80 - Dr / Rx fund
$50 - Haircuts
$80 - Nails
$75 - Auto Fund
$40- Christmas Fund - %

$1350 - TOTAL

14th

$100 - Groceries
$30 - His spending
$60 - Her spending
$60 - His gas
$25 - Her gas
$184 - Auto insurance (4/19)
$75 - Credit Card #2 (4/22)
$175 - Cell Phone (4/22)
$200 - Savings
$40 - Christmas fund - balance
$50 - Birthdays/Special Fund
$25 - Pool Maintenance Fund
$50 - People Fund
$76 - House Maintenance Fund
$200 - Tithe - balance

$1350 - TOTAL

21st

$100 - Groceries
$30 - His spending
$60 - Her spending
$60 - His gas
$25 - Her gas
$675 - Mortgage - %
$260 - Electric (4/26)
$140 - Water bill (5/6)

$1350 - TOTAL

28th

$100 - Groceries
$30 - His spending
$60 - Her spending
$60 - His gas
$25 - Her gas
$1075 - Mortgage - balance (5/1)

$1350 - TOTAL

Notes for May:
Add $ for vacation
Add $ for vet visit

Due Dates:
Mortgage - 1st
Water - 6th
Credit Card #1 - 15th (bal $1200)
Auto Insurance - 19th
Cell Phone - 22nd
Credit Card #2 - 22nd (bal $665)
Electric - 26th

You may be pleasantly surprised to find that you have more than enough money to cover your budget, or you may be devastated to see in black and white exactly how far you are from realistically covering all your needs. Whatever the case, your budget will give you an accurate snapshot and starting point in gaining control over your financial situation. If used consistently, you'll find it to be an invaluable tool and quickly become attached to it.

If you're fortunate enough to learn that you actually operate in the black each month, resist the urge to stray from the structure of the budget. Be disciplined and stick to it! Continue to take only your previously determined weekly spending amount for yourself and put the extra where it's most needed. See what God has to say on the matter and bring your choices to him in prayer. Perhaps there are credit cards you can pay off? Start with the highest interest rate card first and after it's paid to zero, route the money spent on that payment to the next worst offender. Make an effort to pay off your debt as quickly as possible. If credit cards aren't an issue, then perhaps you can work on paying off your autos or even your house. Think big! If you have money left over each month, put it to work for you. Of course, make sure there are funds directed to savings and safe investments too.

Here are a few other ideas:

Are you in a position to take care of much needed home repairs or even, at the expense of sounding a little footloose and fancy free, taking a long overdue vacation? *Everyone* needs a break! We aren't against having fun, we just want you to experience it guilt-free and without a paper trail of debt following behind. Your trip doesn't have to be extravagant; there are many ways to enjoy a fabulous vacation without breaking the piggy bank.

Has participating in a missions trip long tugged at your heart? Maybe this is your time?

Remember that fishing trip or luncheon date that needed to come from your personal spending money? Perhaps you're in a position where you can set aside a few bucks for these pleasures as line items within your monthly budget?

Make a commitment to your financial responsibilities first, and pave the way to enjoying the good stuff, totally guilt-free. If, on the other hand, you now have clarity on just how short you are from making ends meet each month, it's time to get to work. Are there any bills you can reduce or eliminate? Many people, including us, have done away with land lines and use cellular phones exclusively. Can you live without cable? Whether your answer is yes or no, you might need to. Ladies, is it time to give up professional manicures or to start dyeing your hair at home? (Sherry can just see the mouths dropping and hear the audible gasps, but work with me, please!) Eliminating may seem like a step backward, but just the opposite is true. Just as with "less is more," reducing can bring so much *to* the table. Choices! Opportunities! Stress reduction!

Can you negotiate balances or minimum payments with some of your creditors? If you're down to the bare necessities and still aren't cracking the nut, can you manage a part-time job? There are a multitude of ways to earn additional income and a temporary commitment may be a necessary evil. The choices you need to make might not be the most pleasant, but remind yourself that this is a means to a better end and will be well worth it in the long run.

Persevere and be patient. Your future is looking very bright. Implement consistent, strategic changes and soon you'll own everything you purchase outright. Goodbye monthly payments with interest! You'll lay your head on the pillow at night without guilt over unnecessary spending because there isn't any. You'll have pride in how you're managing your finances and delight in the fact they're no longer managing you! Start the work NOW! Make it happen so you can declutter any financial stress and begin reaping the benefits of living within your means. There are countless perks that come along with great decisions and a solid effort: peace of mind, a sense of accomplishment, security, control, and even some unexpected extras. This is just the beginning.

> *"In the house of the wise are stores of choice food and oil,*
>   *but a foolish man devours all he has."*

(Prov. 21:20)

God entrusts us with the responsibility to take care of and be accountable for the blessings he has given us. Do the best you can with what you have.

Beyond the Budget

Building and sticking to a monthly budget is an essential step in your journey toward financial health, but it's just one piece of the puzzle. Here are some down-to-earth, practical tips we've gleaned from our years of growing our fiscal responsibility.

Intentional Spending

Don't carry around large amounts of cash which will just disappear with nothing to show for it, and don't debit purchases unless the money is already accounted for in your budget. If you come across a necessary expense which isn't included in your current monthly expenditures, you may have to make revisions the following month but, until then, remain disciplined and adhere to the plan. Tuck your credit cards away for making reservations and absolute emergencies only! Declutter, folks! We're not here to decide for you what spending should stay and what should go, but if you're going through the effort, do yourself a favor and do it right. If you don't trust your judgment, use someone else's judgment. Sherry used to jokingly tell the boys if they found themselves in a precarious spot: "Use my judgment, not yours!"

Money Talk

If you're married, discuss with your spouse what dollar amount you'll use as the threshold for requiring discussion before purchases. Ours is $25. We each have carte blanche in decision making when it comes to spending money on anything less. Our $25 may sound like a miniscule amount but, oddly enough, we usually even discuss $10 purchases. It's helpful to have a predetermined amount in place to keep us on the same page when we're not with each other. We communicate constantly anyway, so on the front side it's not like we have to go out of our way to talk to each other. On the backside, our agreement saves us from much conflict. It requires us to address everything head on. Perfect!

Proper Planning Prevents Poor Performance

Plan every purchase: *never* purchase without a plan! So many people get in way over their heads with impulsive spending. Avoid becoming a victim of this destructive habit. If you're considering a large purchase, implement a waiting period before allowing yourself to buy the item. This will give you time to research the product, comparison shop, look for sales and, without being driven by emotion, evaluate the financial implications. Lindon likes to ask a question that checks the true cost from a different perspective. "How many hours of work is that purchase costing you?" Evaluating a potential purchase in terms of time versus money will give you a completely different vantage point which may aid your decision making. Implementing a waiting period will, for all intense and purposes, completely eliminate the possibility of impulsive spending. You'll essentially be policing your own spending habits to ensure solid and smart choices.

Stretch the Stretchable

We are huge fans of making the most out of what you have, so why not carry that over to your finances and stretch the spending money you have to the absolute limit too? What do you have to lose? If you have $50 to spend, would you rather purchase $50 worth of products or spend that same $50 and take home products valued at $70, $80, $100 or more? If you're in the mood for a family movie night, would you rather spend $75 to take the family out or just $25—or even less? Here are a few tips that'll make more of a difference than you might ever have imagined.

Real Women (& Men) Coupon

COUPONS, COUPONS, COUPONS! We can't stress this enough. Save and use coupons! There are coupons available for everything from food to household products to clothing to restaurants and so much more. Using coupons is comparable to handing the sales clerk or waitress cash. Why would you pass up free money?

Start with the local newspaper. If you're not a newspaper reader, most companies offer a subscription for a "coupon-filled" Sunday only paper which will cost far less than the all the money you'll be saving. Take the time to clip the coupons. Don't make the mistake, though, of clipping everything; only keep the ones you legitimately need and will use. Warning: just because you have a coupon, doesn't mean you have to use it. Even with a coupon (doubled), some store brands still beat the price. We know people who end up spending far more money with coupons than they ever would have otherwise. They feel compelled to use every coupon they come across, even for products they normally wouldn't buy. If you want to try a new product, a coupon provides a discounted way to give it a go, but stick to what you need and can use.

Check out the online coupons and coupon companies. There are a variety of legitimate sites you can join for a nominal fee. Again, if utilized, you'll save far more than you'll ever spend. These coupon companies not only provide information about sales at your favorite stores, but they pair up the sales with the current coupons offered to maximize your savings. They tell you where to find the coupon, what store to take it to, and what your final price will be. The only thing they don't do is drive you there themselves. It's really a sure thing. We've been behind customers in line who were forced to add to their order during checkout by quickly grabbing a pack of gum or a few candy bars. When their bill was totaled, they were due a refund because the coupons had saved them more than the cost of their purchases. Since stores can't end transactions with a negative total and give customers money back, these customers needed to increase the order total and receive more products for free, just so they could complete their checkout. Doesn't that just sound crazy? And it's all totally legal! If you have no use for the free items, then donate them! Why not? There's an endless need for food donations, and this is a great way to make a contribution.

If you enjoy dining out, consider purchasing an Entertainment Book, which is available for just about every major city in the United States. The book often retails for $35 or so, but just prior to Christmas, there are usually deals available that bring the cost of the book down to $20 or even $15. Many schools or organizations use the Entertainment Book for fundraising projects, and that's a perfect opportunity to help a group make money while saving big bucks in the coming year. You can easily recoup the cost of the book after using just two or three coupons. Not only are there restaurant coupons, but discounts offered for clothing and sporting goods stores and on a myriad of services such as dry cleaning and automobile oil changes. There are savings offered for local entertainment venues such as theaters, bowling alleys, and rock climbing gyms, as well as for out of town attractions, hotel, and travel discounts. If you've never checked out one of these books, you're really missing out. The potential savings are absolutely mindboggling. The key after purchasing the book is to actually remember to use it! As a side note, these books make excellent gifts, especially for college students and young adults who enjoy going out but are (or should be!) on strict budgets. Not only are the savings significant, but we've tried a few new restaurants that we wouldn't have ventured into without the book. Most were delish!

Here's yet another source for coupons. If there are a few favorite shops you frequent, sign up via the store website to be on their email distribution list. Most stores send out weekly or monthly emails with specials and great coupons. We very rarely purchase anything that isn't either on sale or that we don't have a coupon for, or both. With all the deals and incentives available, it makes no sense to do otherwise. The other night we went shopping and bought everything from boots to books to dresses to household items. We had coupons for every single item and saved almost

$200. These were items which needed to be bought one way or the other, and had we not been diligent in watching for sales and collecting coupons, the additional $200 would have been in the retailers' pockets instead of ours. This isn't something our good conscience can allow.

[*Sherry*] I have been working for years on perfecting our shopping for optimal savings and can say that I'm continually blowing my husband away with what we're able to afford and how much we realize in savings. There's definitely a sense of accomplishment and extra gratification when you know you've received the best price possible and can enjoy your purchase all the more.

It *All* Adds Up

What are some other money-saving tips for the ways we spend money every day?

Movies: Except for a really special occasion, skip seeing new release movies in the theater. If you must go, there are a variety of places to score discount ticket pricing. We have a local wholesale warehouse where a pair of movie tickets is sold for $15—a $5 savings off the regular box office price. One of our theaters offers a customer loyalty souvenir cup. After the initial $5 cup purchase, unlimited refills are just $1 each for the remainder of the year. This has saved us BIG money! Does your community have a local "dollar theater"? They're more like $3 or $4 theaters now, but the savings are still substantial. Be forewarned though, they make up their money at the concession stand, and $20 or $30 can be spent in a heartbeat. We're not advocating for breaking any rules but will tell you that a $1 box of red vines or junior mints can fit nicely into an average-sized purse. Did we just say that? Or better yet, what about a movie night at home? The $1 box movies that can be rented now at just about every grocery store and gas station are a great choice for family movie night. We invested $20 in an old-fashioned popcorn popper and have a fantastic time when all the kids (who are all over 21) are sacked out in the living room, watching movies with us, and munching on snacks.

Lunches: Do you purchase your lunch every day while at work? STOP! Perhaps limit your lunch purchases to once a week and bring your lunch from home on the other days. Packing a sandwich or leftovers can save your wallet $30 or more a week; it all adds up fast. Does your office have a microwave? Even a $2 frozen meal is more cost efficient than eating out, and if you choose carefully, it won't compromise your waistline either!

Books: Are you an avid reader? Don't buy books that will just collect dust and never get referenced (unlike *Declutter Now!*) after your initial read. Patronize your local library. Sometimes we forget the endless resources they offer at absolutely no charge. Books, magazines, and even DVD rentals for free. If you haven't been to your library in a while, it's time to check it out. Many libraries also lend books that you can download to your e-reader.

Groceries: You've heard this over and over again, don't shop hungry. It's great advice! Go to the grocery store like a person on a mission. Have a list, coupons in hand, and take care of business. The more structured and prepared you are, the less chance you'll have for impulsive buying. Discipline and timing are key here.

These practical tips are just the beginning. You probably have a few of your own already, and will continue to collect them from friends, co-workers, magazine articles, television shows, etc. The bottom line—and it's altogether possible—is to:

Share the Wealth

We've been focused thus far in sharing how to cut corners and what not to spend on. It's time to shift gears and discuss some areas we find deserving of your financial contribution. You might have wondered why we left "Tithe" and "People Fund" in our mock budget blank, with no dollar amounts. We did that intentionally so we could explain later. Let's start with tithing.

The Call to Tithe

Tithing is a controversial topic to be sure. Pastors often dread teaching on it and congregants usually cringe when the topic comes up. Many people believe the Bible is crystal clear that tithing is required, but then question if it means 10% of their gross or net income. Others believe the Bible never makes this assertion and Christians have misconstrued the original intent. We aren't going to debate the controversy. What we hope to impress upon you is if you feel called by God to tithe, treat it as much of a priority as your mortgage payment or medical insurance is. This isn't something you can be lukewarm about. If you're not sure how you feel about tithing, take the time to read and research. Either way, this is a very important decision and deserves your time and attention. Have an educated opinion on the matter, and if you feel called to tithe, then make it happen.

We believe there are a variety of ways to answer God's call on our lives and to be obedient in tithing is just one of them. For us, it's a combination of giving our money, time, gifts, talents, etc. I [Lindon] believe in "miracles in the mailbox." God expects us to give him our firsts, whether tithing or otherwise, and he tells us we should expect miracles in our lives in return. Don't be afraid to give up your best to God because he will always one-up you with something better. I have always been amazed by how true this is and how faithful God is. Whenever I'm in need, or whenever I feel I may have given up something valuable, I always receive more than I gave and more than I ever expected to receive. Miracles just arrive in one way or the other, and often they've been delivered to my mailbox. God is good, but you have to give him room to work in your life. Bring him your firsts and, in his time, he'll take care of the rest. As Proverbs 3:9-10 says: "Honor the Lord with your wealth, with the first fruits of all your crops; then your barns will be filled to overflowing, and your vats will brim over with new wine."

People Fund

Together, we've created a People Fund which has brought us an indescribable amount of joy. This is a fund we dip into when we come across someone in need. It's a line item in our budget and we accumulate it monthly. We desired to be in a position to help when instances present themselves, and we needed a plan so our budget could back up our hearts. Wouldn't it be nice to know when one of those moments presents itself, without hesitation, you can offer help and make a difference? We have used money from our People Fund to help family, offered anonymous assistance to friends, and sometimes even strangers, donated to diaper and backpack drives at our church, purchased turkey dinners at Thanksgiving, etc. If it's appropriate, we share with the recipient about our People Fund. Our intention is not to gain credit or recognition, but in the hopes our giving will be multiplied when the recipients create their own People Fund someday to help others. Whether you put away $10 or $100 per month, we encourage you to give it a try. It's the best feeling in the world to be prepared to help when your heart tugs at you.

Review, Revise and Repair

There's one small task you can perform annually which will make a big difference in ensuring your efforts have maximum payoff. Declutter your credit report! As of this writing, current laws allow for one free credit report from each of the three credit bureaus per person per year. Check out www.annualcreditreport.com. If you haven't done this before, it's time you do it now! You might be shocked to discover credit reports aren't always accurate. We've each discovered wrong addresses and employers listed against our reports. There have been inaccuracies with regard to balances and payment histories, and outstanding doctor bills we didn't know we had. There can be negative reporting which should have automatically fallen off after a certain time period, but the "automatic" part wasn't so automatic. You might find debt on your report that isn't even yours. It's critical to go through every line on your report and check for inaccuracies and, just as important, to get them fixed. The report will provide instructions for submitting corrections and disputes, so check it out and feel confident in having another area of your life decluttered.

Living to Tell about It

You've probably caught on by now that we aren't "get rich quick" or gimmick-driven people and, perhaps much to your chagrin, we haven't proposed an effortless and painless way to the top. We're advocates for hard work, diligent effort, and disciplined structure, have lived it in more ways than you can count, and have survived to tell about it! You can depend on us for sage advice. We've each navigated through extremely difficult financial times and have implemented strategies to cope and survive. Here are a couple of stories which will give you a glimpse of our personal experiences.

[Sherry] When I was running a single parent household, I ran a tight financial ship with few exceptions allowed or even possible. One of my rules was I permitted myself a certain amount of cash each week for spending money, and when the cash ran out, so did my spending. End of story! One night I was driving around with my boys, who were about 12 and 14 at the time, and one of them mentioned that ice cream sounded good. I knew I didn't have any cash, and I was dead set against using my debit card, even if the tab was only going to be a few bucks. A few bucks here and a few bucks there…it all adds up, and I learned it was easier and safer simply not to stray.

I must admit, though, ice cream did sound pretty good on a hot Phoenix summer night. So what to do? I told the boys if they could find enough change in my truck for ice cream, we'd get some. You have no idea the madness that ensued! I pulled into a local drive-in and my boys began to take apart my entire truck. They looked under every mat and cushion, tore apart my glove box, and rummaged through my console. I went on an excavation mission, digging into the depths of my purse. When we were done, we'd amassed almost $3.00 and hoped it would be enough for three ice cream cones. After we ordered, we held our breath and waited for the total with tax: $2.83! We made it! We started cheering and hootin' and hollerin' and high-fiving each other. I'm sure the fast food worker on the other end of the intercom thought we were absolutely nuts, and we felt a little nuts, but we also felt pretty darn good! Those were the best ice cream cones we ever had. We enjoyed them enormously and didn't compromise any financial guidelines that I had in place. It was nothing short of glorious!

[*Lindon*] When I was going through my divorce, I was more financially upside down than I'd ever been in my life. You know the times when you wonder if God may have finally given you more than you can handle. This was definitely a concern for me. The lucrative job I had was gone; the company I loved closed its doors and I was out of work. My house had been emptied of just about everything I'd ever owned, and life as I knew it was gone forever. As tough as it was, my kids had decided to still live with me, and I knew I had to implement a strategic game plan, and fast, to survive.

I started filling out applications, one after the other, until I'd filled out 214 applications. This is no exaggeration. I finally landed a good job with a reputable company but at a salary that was $47K less a year than what I'd previously earned. Talk about a humbling reality check, but it was all I had, and I was willing to take it and make it work. Something was better than nothing! I've always operated under the belief that it's easier to find a job when you have a job, so even if this job didn't grow into a long- term career opportunity, at least it would keep me going, barely, until I could find something better.

In order to make ends meet, it was critical I make changes—and fast. I turned off the cable service to the house and shut off my cell phone service. I replaced my electric dryer with a gas model which saved almost $60 per month on my utility bill. I appreciate a well-landscaped and maintained yard but cut my watering back from daily to every third day or so—a huge concession for me. All exterior decorative lights were turned off; only the porch lights were left on. The insurance on my two old pick-up trucks was reduced to just liability. Eating out was a luxury and, aside from the infrequent $6-$8 fast food meals, the kids and I only splurged on pizza once during the first year. Credit card payments were reduced to the barest of minimums, and I cut up my debit card. It's easy to spend more money than you realize with a debit card and I wasn't going to take that chance. I even moved my computer out of the office and into my bedroom. By doing this, I could seal off the office and save the cost of heating and cooling an additional room. My truck payment was always made on time. No vehicle, no job.

Unfortunately, no matter how hard I tried, I wasn't able to take care of everything and, ultimately, I lost my home. The mortgage payment was completely unrealistic with my new wage, and I had to accept that fate. While I wasn't able to keep my home, I slept at night knowing I'd done everything possible within my power. I might have lost my home, but my self-respect was intact. The importance of this cannot be understated.

While these are only two examples among plenty from our lives, we want to instill confidence there is a lifetime of reality-based experience and wisdom behind our advice, and most importantly, there is hope through the lean times. Lindon always says, "This too shall pass." And one of Sherry's favorite bumper stickers is: "Tough times don't last but tough people do!" Both are true. But remember, at some point during the tough times, you must implement positive, effective change to transform your hopes into reality.

Timeless Advice

First Timothy 6:7-10 says, "For we brought nothing into the world, and we can take nothing out of it. But if we have food and clothing, we will be content with that. People who want to get rich fall into temptation and a trap and into many foolish and harmful desires that plunge men into ruin and destruction. For the love of money is a root of all kinds of evil. Some people, eager for money, have wandered from the faith and pierced themselves with many griefs."

Paul blames money for so much…or is it truly the money he blames? Read the passage again and pinpoint who Paul is actually pointing his finger at. People! It's the desires of people that are the underlying problem. We love the message that Paul tried fervently to convey and continually marvel at how advice given so many years ago still holds abundantly true today. Obviously, money is necessary. We need to pay our mortgages, put food on the table and gas in the car. We all have needs; how we manage with what we have will determine our success or failure.

It Takes Heart

Since we've attempted to present a comprehensive, clear approach to decluttering, it may sound odd when we suggest following our advice to a "T" still won't be enough. How can we expect something more from you when we haven't even instructed you on what it is? Kind of sounds like the crazy English teacher from your high school freshman class, doesn't it? Well, not necessarily!

People, we beg of you, implore you, to bring your heart and best effort to this. This is something we can't force on you; it must come from within. The financial decluttering you're planning to do must go hand in hand with an entirely new mindset and, for some, a completely different lifestyle. It must permeate all your day-to-day thoughts, actions, and decisions. It's been said that it takes just thirty days to break an old habit or create a new one. Isn't thirty days of serious work worth a lifelong payoff? You can't possibly experience all the blessings God has in store if you're weighed down by the dollars and cents of the world. The problem is most people are so accustomed to inviting financial demands, obligations, and burdens into their lives, they don't realize the negative impact they have, not to mention the tremendous adverse domino effect on other areas as well. You may not get how radically your lives would improve overall and, if you don't get it, what would motivate you to work toward it? This is where a little trust and faith come in handy. Follow our thought process for a moment.

A Love Story

This journey, in a sense, is an affair of the heart—an affair that you're allowed, and absolutely encouraged, to have! Start with some simple flirting. (OK, this is cheesy, but humor us!) Use the simple, practical approaches we've shared to aid you in getting control of your budget, reducing expenses, and curbing spending habits. You'll feel good about yourself and build some confidence. Then work your way up to dating. Perhaps find creative ways to cut corners with coupons and specials. Enjoy the pleasures you desire, but in such a way that allows you to feel good about it. No guilt! There's definitely something to be said for getting an out-of-this-world deal. Are you starting to feel a twinge of excitement? Motivation?

The serious courting starts and you find you have a much more optimistic view of things. The responsibility level you're exhibiting feels good. Real good. You have a new sense of purpose and accomplishment. Then comes the real commitment. People talk about the old ball and chain. Well, financial bondage is literally just that, but it's gone! No ball and chain for you. No sireee! You've worked your way through to a new kind of marriage, one that brings you a level of peace and freedom you've never before known! Ah, and the pleasures this marriage brings? WOWZER!

Just to tantalize you a bit, think about purchasing that new suit or watch you've been admiring, the laptop you've legitimately needed for close to forever, or the fancy kitchen mixer you've been eyeing to support your cooking and baking habit. Think about how it would feel to pay cash for items like these and own them before they ever make it home and through your front door. No credit cards, no monthly payments due long after you made the initial purchase, and no regret. Are you now beginning to see the correlation?

Marrying Financial Freedom–for God

Let's take it one step further. What else can freedom from financial bondage bring you? The freedom to experience God's will in your life! Imagine having the finances and ability to do the work God is calling you to do, when he calls you. Wouldn't it be nice to be ready and able to go? God longs for you to be in this place and he's equipped you with the tools, but you have to do the work to get there. He's waiting for you!

Depending on your current financial situation, you may have a long road to recovery ahead or you might already be on the right track. Make a decision to declutter financially so you'll free up the resources needed to seek the true desires of your heart and answer any call God makes. Be ready! The preparation alone will unite you in a marriage with financial freedom you can be proud of, and that's just the beginning of the honeymoon.

Chapter 4

If the Buck Stops, What Can You Start?

AHHHHH, THE DESIRE AND PRESSURE to have a big fat paycheck, a snazzy sports car, Italian tailored suits, expensive watches, trendy pumps, designer handbags, and the most up-to-date technology for all your electronic communication and organizational needs. It's a race to the top, clawing and fighting your way, oblivious to the losses you accumulate, with the focus only on the end result—the big corner office, the power title on the door nameplate, and the paycheck which allows you to compete in the big leagues. Is your drive fueled by passion for your purpose or merely the digits on your paycheck and the status you desire to obtain?

While your career climb may not be the white-collar professional path, the same misguided ambition can be present in any job. Construction foremen are consumed with driving the biggest, *baddest* trucks around, the cost of them even rivaling the office execs' BMWs. Each industry has its top dogs, the bar to hit, the co-worker to outshine, and the bigger salary beckoning. Sometimes the motivation appears more honorable as with the workaholic parent who is sacrificing everything to provide for the family. Regardless of the intent, the losses accrued can provide the same damaging end results. Ask yourself the million dollar questions. Is what my family and I give up worth what we're gaining? Am I following God's will for my life or putting my desires ahead of his?

Society has been brainwashed to believe external influences will ensure our happiness. A full head of hair will give men the lifestyle they desire, and the new body-shaping wrap will snag any woman the greatest guy on the planet. The same holds true with financial success. How many advertising dollars are spent on get-rich-quick infomercials which suggest money and happiness are one in the same? Do you buy into this? If so, is this how it should be? Is money the end-all in your measure of success? When you hand someone your business card, how important is the title printed under your name? Is your motivation in the desire to wear the role of big-shot like a badge of honor? Is it to one-up your competition, or even your co-workers? Is the victory in continually striving to meet the demands of a "more and better" lifestyle? Is the drive simply powered by the need to keep up with a totally mismanaged and out of control budget? Do you operate in fear or guilt mode and believe anything less than a twelve-hour workday is falling short? Be truthful with yourself when considering these critical questions. An honest assessment is the best first step in decluttering your career life, and your livelihood depends on it.

We are prepared to suggest, and argue on behalf of, what we believe true success in your career should look like. You may have already surmised that it's nothing like the images conjured up when reading the previous questions. We fear that, more often than not, people are caught up chasing the wrong goals and lose out on reaping the benefits and rewards which bring true joy and fulfillment.

As you delve into this chapter, you'll begin to see pieces of the three previous chapters melding into one. This is a critical part of the entire decluttering process. Often, the same tips and tools we share for decluttering one area can easily be applied to another, and this is precisely what will equip you to deal with clutter challenges not specifically addressed in this book. Hard as we try, it would be impossible to cover every topic worthy of decluttering, so always be on the lookout for any practical application opportunities you encounter. In no time at all, this mode of operation will be the norm and come naturally in any situation.

Advice in Action

The rough draft of this particular chapter was written months ago, and yesterday we decided it was time to dig back in and start the editing process. As we began, we realized that God's amazing orchestration had been hard at work in our lives during the interim, and we hadn't even realized it. We're always excited to use and share the principles we believe in and relish God's timing and wisdom for this latest opportunity.

Lindon keeps tabs on current job openings and frequently sends out resumes. A couple of weeks ago he received a response for a very promising position within a well-established company. The interview process moved forward at lightning speed. We've found that typically companies are taking a month or two just to review a resume, but this company was far from the norm. We were blown away when they called and scheduled Lindon's initial phone interview within twenty-four hours of their first contact with him. They meant business! Next, a face to face interview was held, then another phone interview, and finally one last in-person meeting. All of this took place within a week, which was unprecedented to say the least. He was offered the job and, with some reservation, accepted. The company was headquartered in Phoenix, so Lindon would be working at corporate headquarters, the perfect setting for rubbing shoulders and getting to know the "mucky-mucks." The position offered significant potential and new challenges. It got him out of banking (good), but kept him in a call center (not so good). The job would require a longer commute and likely longer hours, at least initially. He would realize a pay increase from his current salary, but the money didn't seem to influence him as it would have in years past. His paid time off would be substantially less, and there would be a delay in its onset. Back and forth he went; back and forth we went. It was a week from you know where. Definitely one of the hardest decisions Lindon has had to make, and he didn't let Sherry off the hook from participating in the debate and discussions. It was exhausting!

Finally, at the eleventh hour, Lindon withdrew his application and decided to stay in his current job with the caveat, for his dear wife's benefit, that he would *stop looking* and stay put for at least two years. His current job, while not as much money as he's capable of earning and not exactly what he enjoys doing, meets our financial needs and affords us the lifestyle we enjoy so much. We have time to spend together, time to write, time to help others, time for the boat! We'll have the time to fly to Trent's USAF boot camp and S.E.R.E. graduations, and the flexibility to schedule events to promote our book.

The same day Lindon decided against the job, he called our pastor and let him know we would be ready, willing, and able to make a commitment to host small group in our home each week for the next year, something we'd been asked to pray about. We had doubted we could manage hosting if Lindon was juggling the demands of a new job, but since that wasn't in the equation any longer, we jumped at the chance to serve. We had prayed for God's direction in our decision making, and we believed that he spoke.

Divine intervention was even more apparent after Lindon's current manager made an unscheduled trip to Phoenix on the day after the withdrawal of the application. His manager shared with him plans to develop and enlarge the department he worked in. They would need his help interviewing and hiring dozens of new people, and they even mentioned a potential management opening for which he was perfectly qualified. It would be in the same convenient location with the same perfect work schedule and benefits. There were no guarantees the opportunity would actually transpire, of course, but the possibility was there, and it reaffirmed to Lindon that he'd made the right decision for the right reasons.

It took a weeklong deliberation for us to realize the decision wasn't to be based on a bigger salary or the opportunity to climb up the corporate ladder. It boiled down to making sure we protected time for our quality of life; for the activities which were most important to us as a couple and family. Sure, it's flattering to have a company pursue and want you, to show excitement in having you on board. It isn't always easy to give up the big, or at least bigger bucks, and it's tough to pass on an offer which feels ripe with opportunity. For a young gun, this may have been the ideal break but, for Lindon, it wasn't where he felt led. I [Sherry] am proud of him for listening to God's will and having the strength and sense to follow his direction, not necessarily choosing what *seemed* to be the obvious answer.

Responsibility Reigns

When President Harry Truman placed the words, "the buck stops here" on his desk, he wasn't talking about an actual greenback, of course. He was speaking of responsibility. He was tired of everyone passing the buck and neglecting their responsibilities. Truman was determined to initiate a new era where problems were actually solved and not just left for the next victim.

There's a lot to be said for responsibility. We are called to be responsible to God, our family, our friends, our jobs, and ourselves, but the act of being responsible isn't a simple task. It encompasses so much, including how we care for and treat people, the decisions we make, and the character and integrity with which we live our lives, just to highlight a few of the heavy hitters. Being responsible affects every area of our being, including our career choices and work environment, and this will be the next road we travel down in the journey toward total decluttering.

Proverbs 11:4 is the perfect starting point for our discussion: "Wealth is worthless in the day of wrath, but righteousness delivers from death." When you are standing before God on judgment day, no amount of money is going to buy your way into heaven. It's worthless at that point. All that will matter is how responsible you've been in your obedience to God and in your response to what he's called upon you to do with your life. Sobering thought, isn't it? You've got to make the right decisions *now*, ahead of time, because when you're standing before God, there won't be time for a re-do. Just like quitting a nicotine habit *after* being diagnosed with cancer, the devastating damage is already done.

Hearing God's Heart

Consider Proverbs 11:2, "When pride comes, then comes disgrace, but with humility comes wisdom," and Proverbs 16:18, "Pride goes before destruction, a haughty spirit before a fall." How about Jeremiah 9:23-24, which wraps up all of the above. "This is what the Lord says: 'Let not the wise man boast of his wisdom or the strong man boast of his strength or the rich man boast of his riches, but let him who boasts boast about this: that he understands and knows me, that I am the Lord, who exercises kindness, justice and righteousness on earth, for in these I delight,' declares the Lord."

Focusing on money for any reason, being prideful, arrogant, or conceited—God hates it all. He is crystal clear on this. He's not the least bit impressed by your paycheck, job title, or office size. He doesn't delight in the person who gives up the right stuff to chase the wrong, even with good intention. It could say #1 Street Sweeper after your name and that wouldn't mean any more or less to God than Nuclear Physicist. We think it's fair to say he's most concerned with the heart and motivation behind your actions and accomplishments, your integrity and character, service to others, obedience to his word, devotion to your family, and love for him.

The choices you make in your job or with your career, and living in God's will, may seem unrelated at first but we believe there's a definite correlation. Most people spend more time at work than they do in any other single area of their life. The emphasis is often centered around how much you earn, rather than on how much you give. The pursuit of the power title tends to overshadow the importance of the work being done. The finances you have to manage, the insurance you are able to utilize, and the time available for vacations are all dictated by your job. The fear you live with may hinder you from trusting God and relying on him. Influences from your career and job have the potential to trip you up big time and the necessity to make responsible, Christ-centered decisions in this area cannot be understated. Since these choices directly impact every other part of your life, the link is undeniable.

Money Misconceptions

We aren't naïve. We're aware the norm is "money makes the world go round" and status and power are worshipped, but that doesn't mean we have to agree or conform. In our society, money is a necessity, but where it falls in the pecking order of priority in your life is up to you. Not too many people would consider working for a company if they weren't getting paid what they thought they were worth. Just because they wouldn't, however, doesn't mean it may not be the right thing to do. The standard dictates there is a relevant and significant connection between your job and your income, but we aren't convinced there should be. What if your job duties bring you deep gratification? Do you have the pleasure of making a positive difference in the lives of others? Perhaps your schedule compliments the demands of your family time and life? Maybe the benefits and perks of your job allow for important relationships or ministry work. Money is not the end-all and shouldn't be given the top spot it often receives. Suggesting this might appear a ludicrous philosophy, but we're certain enough in what we believe to do just that. Perhaps that value you place on your job should be more centered on what it's worth to you in non-monetary ways. Wouldn't it be a wonderful world if you could actually put the joys of your heart before the pursuit of the dollar? The truth is, you can!

We are by no means promoting financial negligence, and we absolutely understand there can be legitimate reasons why your career may have to come first, for a very short time. We wish to stress, however, the importance of decluttering any imprudent career choices, no matter what they are fueled by. Reevaluate your situation and do everything within your power and means to make sure your priorities are in order. You may have to be patient, make sacrifices, or navigate through uncomfortable territory, but ask God to reveal what needs to stop in your job and start in your life.

Twisting Truman

Let's twist Truman's intent just a bit. Let's say the buck, as in the actual dollar, does stop here. It's been said that when money speaks, the truth keeps silent. Since we are seeking truth, perhaps it's prudent that we silence money. For a moment, devalue the significance of your income and career climb, and concentrate on what makes you truly happy and what you would delight in for your future. If the buck stops, meaning any misguided significance you've placed on money or career-related matters is removed, what starts? Pause and ponder that for a moment. If the focus isn't on the wrong priorities, you have the freedom and ability to shift that energy—to what? Are you so caught up in the status quo that you don't allow yourself to consider anything else? Close your eyes, step outside the box, and dream a little. The answers you unveil may truly surprise you. For us, we have a huge desire to serve, to make a difference in hearts and lives, so this is our starting point for finding more meaning and satisfaction in our existence.

What starts here? Our MINISTRY starts here!

If we had the choice, we would both gladly give up our day jobs and serve in a ministry capacity full time. We'd write a book, tour to promote it, and then write some more! As with most, though, we have a house to run, debts to pay, obligations to meet, along with a zillion other hurdles. The obvious question is how in the world do you get from where you are to where you want to be? This is where the implementation of different decluttering strategies will pay off.

We began with the decision to declutter our finances. We feel it's

healthier not to have career decisions governed either by earning potential or financial requirements, so reducing our need is a sensible first step.
This is the heart behind what we profess. By following the same steps
we outlined for you, we set ourselves up to reduce our overhead and our
financial need. We have a game plan to pay off our current debt as quickly
as possible, thereby putting ourselves in an optimal financial position for
working toward our goal. Then if we're fortunate enough to be able to
step away from our current full-time jobs to pursue writing and promoting, we want to be well prepared to go.

The next hurdle was finding the time to write; we had to declutter
our schedule. Like you, we are busy. Aside from work, which consumes
40-45 hours per week of each of our lives, we have house upkeep, physical exercise, church commitments, family time, doctor visits, parties and
social time, service obligations, and of course "us" time. (We're still hon-
eymooning!) If we seriously wanted to write a book, twenty minutes
here and there was just not going to cut it. We've had to make a serious
effort at nailing down writing time. Weekday mornings before work,
evenings after our walk, taking the laptop on road trips, and saying no
to invitations we would have liked to accept were part of the deal. Even
though decluttering finances is difficult, at least it's tangible. Decluttering
and adjusting your lifestyle to accommodate goals can be a little trickier.
It hasn't been easy, but we feel good about what we're doing, and even
though we may miss out occasionally, we know God has us where he
wants us.

After we finish the book, who will look at it? Decluttering our minds
was key to being released from the bondage of self-doubt and any self-
defeating behavior. We've never published anything before, don't have
impressive degrees, and are not officially working in any area of ministry.

Having a book published might end up being nothing more than a pipe dream. Will all of our hard work and sacrifice be for nothing? No! Definitely not! But we had to come to terms with this. When we started *Declutter Now!* we knew it was at God's urging and, whether it was for an audience of three (God and us!) or many, many more, we'll have no regrets because it brings us joy and we believe it to be God's will. Hard to argue with that, isn't it?

There will be more decluttering along the way, but for us, decluttering our finances, schedules, and stinkin' thinkin' were the biggies. The reality is that getting from A to B is often more of a process than an easy one-step task, but if you never start the process, you'll never arrive at your destination. Break down your challenge into manageable chunks and, with steadfast determination, meet the obstacles head on, one by one.

We hold to the belief that if you're doing what you feel led to do and, more importantly, what God is calling you to do, not only will you realize tremendous personal satisfaction and joy, the monetary buck that's needed will find its way to you as well.

Are You at a Crossroad?

We all know family and friends who are unhappy at work. They might make great money, but they dread getting up each morning and are unfulfilled in what they do; they are often just plain miserable. Their status title is on the door, but they've spent years on a particular career path and feel more boxed in than accomplished. They fear it's not possible to make the change their heart desires because they can't afford to start all over again. Even if they could survive a substantial pay cut to switch gears, they may not have the time and funds required for the requisite education. Perhaps the financial potential isn't promising in the field that their dreams are made of. Maybe their spouse is unsupportive and prefers the status quo or, even more damaging, is content to have their worker bee slaving away 24/7, while they're home being irresponsible with the money earned and living the high life. They're spinning their wheels in a dead end job and enduring a never-ending cycle of doing, doing, doing, and going, going, going, to keep up with a lifestyle they no longer want (or to keep up with the Joneses next door). We bet there are a few people whom come to mind right away. Perhaps you are even seeing yourself somewhere in this picture? Sadly, we've both been there ourselves. There are many reasons we stay, but money and position are two tempting seductions that lead the pack.

An old pastor friend of Lindon's once told him that if you're not appreciated for what you bring to your position and to the business, you need to diligently seek out a company that will appreciate you. How many knowingly accept so much less than this standard? They settle and sell themselves out because their priorities aren't in order, or they aren't willing to do the work to make changes desperately needed. Maybe they're afraid to make those changes.

What about the small business entrepreneur who must work ninety hours per week to get her business off the ground? The owner who can't afford to hire the help he needs so he is relegated to doing it all by himself? These people have an extra layer of responsibility. Not only do they fear making the bills at home, but the bills at work are their responsibility too. So they worry twice as much—at least!

We have both owned our own businesses and understand the sacrifice it takes. We aren't against business ownership by any means, but we aren't convinced it's right for everyone. A lot depends on the industry you choose, the commitment it requires, your level of discipline, your life stage, and what your priorities and responsibilities are outside of work.

So, what to do if you're at a crossroad and have come to the conclusion it's time to make some critical changes. How do you attempt to change a situation which seems to have insurmountable odds against you? This is where you must dig deep and transition from being in the wrong place for the wrong reasons, to stepping over the line and starting on the road to the joy and freedom waiting for you. What would you choose for a career even if you weren't going to make a dime from it? If there was no compensation other than the pleasure and satisfaction you earn in your job, where would you be? Start your journey with the basic realization your life shouldn't be driven by the dollar nor success measured by a paycheck. When the real "buck" isn't money, but what makes you tick, it opens up a whole world of hope and potential for genuine satisfaction that far surpasses the temporal and surface high of the dollar sign. Are you prepared to start? This isn't a journey for the fragile or tentative; you must be willing and certain. If it's time for a shift in direction, however, we pray God would ready your heart and propel you forward with absolute confidence.

What starts here? Your NEW OUTLOOK starts here!

Job Satisfaction

When you're evaluating your current career path, there are many telling questions you can ask yourself:

- Does it bring you joy? This isn't often the first question someone might ask when inquiring about your job, but it should be!
- Are you where you want to be?

- Does your job provide the necessary means to support the lifestyle you've determined is appropriate?
- Is there enough time for your spouse and kids? Enough time for the activities you enjoy?
- Is your job fulfilling, and does it satisfy your passions and interests?
- Are the hours conducive to the schedule you want to keep? Lindon's grandfather used to say that if you aren't doing it in forty [hours], then you're doing something wrong. There's wisdom in that. We each only get so much time. Are you using your forty in the best way possible?

If the answers to the above questions are yes, then congratulations! You are in a small minority of people who are actually happy and satisfied with their jobs and are where they should be. Keep doing what you're doing, and do it well so your chance of retaining your position is high. No matter how good your job is, always have a Plan B and, if you're an overachiever, a Plan C & D too. Today any company, big or small, new or old, is at risk for failure or reorganization. With competition so fierce, many companies are replacing older, higher-salaried workers with those who will accept a much lower wage. Although they lose some experience and wisdom with this practice, in order to keep the doors open or fatten their wallets, many owners are willing to make such changes. The current economy is forcing companies to increase profit by downsizing and cutbacks. And, unfortunately, anyone can have an accident or unexpected health problem which permanently alters their future. You can't prepare or plan for every circumstance, but by having a realistic view of what you bring to the table and what your options are in case of the unforeseen, you'll be way ahead of the game should quick decisions need to be made.

What starts here? Your BACKUP PLAN starts here!

Work to Do

If you answered the questions in the previous section with an abundance of "no's," you've got some work to do, perhaps literally. Evaluate exactly which part of your job you're unhappy with. Is it the right career field but the wrong company? Is your career path totally off the mark and you regret all the time wasted not following your true aspiration? Do you spend far too much time commuting, or are you working an excessive number of hours? Does your forty end up being sixty or more? Determine what needs to be changed and create a plan to make it happen. Yes, the concept is ridiculously simple—change what you don't like. We also agree that the actual implementation is often far more difficult than the concept. You're probably already saying, "Yeah, right, if it was only that easy…" Consider this. Simple or challenging will have precisely the same end result, absolutely nothing will ever change, if you don't create a plan of action and put it in motion.

Have you ever wandered into a consignment craft store? If you're like me [*Sherry*], you look at the projects and think that many of them wouldn't be hard to make. Why would you spend more money to purchase something, which may not even be exactly what you want, when you could construct it for less yourself and design it precisely to your specs? The truth of the matter is you may never actually go to a craft supply store, purchase the material and any tools needed, carve out the time to make it, and actually put it all together. It's easy to look at the end result and have confidence that you could and would make it happen.

Perhaps it truly would be easy to make. But, if you don't follow through, it can be the easiest task in the world and you'll never accomplish it. Let's say you're totally inspired and actually go to the store and buy all the materials, only to have them sit in your home and collect dust. You've then not only wasted time and money but also lost what you attempted to save in the first place, making the scenario even more insulting. It might have been a great idea, but if you don't see it through to fruition, you'll end up with nothing but a waste of time and money and a lingering feeling of failure.

Apply this to your career aspirations. If you truly desire to make a change but don't put an action plan in place and move on it, you'll never craft your life's project and future. You may as well succumb to purchasing the item as-is off the store shelf, which comes at a premium price. It may not be exactly what you want, but heck, you settle for it anyway. This equates to giving up and accepting whatever your current circumstances are, instead of pooling your resources, creating your own unique combination of success, and controlling the direction and outcome. Perhaps you've begun collecting the material you'll need. You've researched job markets and companies of interest, considered some adjustments that would have to be made, purchased reading material for your exploration, and have had a few "ah-ha" moments which gave you a temporal high, but you never executed your design. The pieces of your project are strewn about unfinished. Don't let this be a wasted opportunity.

Teresa, a friend of Sherry's, made a point years back which significantly impacted Sherry's outlook. Forty-three at the time, Teresa was considering completely changing her career path by going to nursing school. She pondered if it was worth it, at her age, to invest four or five years of her life into school and finally concluded that, God willing, she would be forty-eight then one way or the other. Would she rather be forty-eight *with* a degree in the career field she desperately desired or forty-eight *without* one? Rhetorical indeed, but asking the question made the point Teresa needed to hear. She's now a happy, successful RN, working on the cardio floor of a hospital right around the corner. Go Tere!

What starts here? Your ACTION PLAN and FOLLOW THROUGH start here!

Getting Started

What if your motivation matches your desire but significant changes aren't possible at present? Even if patience isn't your forte, remain positive and progressive during the interim and remind yourself the best is yet to come. Make the most you can with what you have and never lose sight of your goals and plan. Transitions often require many pieces fitting together and, even in the best case scenario, this won't happen all at once. Implementing small but instrumental parts of a bigger, better plan will keep your faith alive during the waiting period. Attitude is everything and the right one, coupled with perseverance, can make or break your success.

If you're miserable in your current position but have to stay put for a while longer, there's no reason to dread each day. Quite the contrary! You have vision and hope of something better, and while waiting, there are tasks to be done that will pave the way to your future. You know the saying, "Just a spoonful of sugar…" It's so true! Make this a time of joyful rejuvenation and lighten up any delays with activities that are progressive and encouraging. As you brainstorm and plan your career decluttering, write your ideas down and make a to-do list. What's it going to take to get from where you are to where you want to be? Spend time researching the educational path or training required. What financial aids are available to you? Establish a specific and realistic timeline in plotting your path. Can you declutter your finances and change your lifestyle so your needs are less? What other obstacles must be overcome?

Make a list you can check off as you accomplish tasks leading you closer to your goal. (It's been over a year since creating their vision board and they just made the purchase they'd been desiring! Way to go guys!) Nicole, our daughter-in-law, just made a vision board for her and Trent's fridge. There's something they want to purchase but aren't in a position to do so quite yet, so she put a collage of pictures together to remind them of their goal. They see this board daily and are continually reminded of the goal. Incorporate some creative and motivational aids to keep you going in the right direction. And, of course, don't forget the power of prayer. Bathe yourself in prayer and positive reinforcement through Scripture. You'll find there are a plethora of verses on hope. Here are a few to get you started:

> *"'For I know the plans I have for you,' declares*
> *the Lord, 'plans to prosper you and not to harm*
> *you, plans to give you hope and a future.'"*
>
> (Jer. 29:11)

> *"And hope does not disappoint us, because God has poured out his*
> *love into our hearts by the Holy Spirit, whom he has given to us"*
>
> (Rom. 5:5).

"But those who hope in the Lord will renew their strength.
They will soar on wings like eagles; they will run and
not grow weary, they will walk and not be faint"

(Isa. 40:31).

Lean on the Lord during these times, and pray for your hope to stay strong and your plans to come to fruition. And while you may need patience, by all means, don't pray for it! The old saying goes that if you pray for patience, God will answer by providing tribulation to work through because that is the way you learn to be patient. Definitely stick to prayers of hope!

If you're going to have to walk down a particular path, even an undesirable one, there are ways to make it more palatable and even enjoyable. You can do more than just grit your teeth and bear it. Make an intentional effort to surround yourself, from the inside out, with a positive spirit. It's not worth wasting your time and energy on anything that doesn't benefit your heart and life!

What starts here? Your HOPE and GOOD ATTITUDE start here!

Tips on Tolerating

[*Lindon*] I have some helpful tips for tolerating your work environment while you're preparing to make a change. Suggesting this may sound terrible, but it's a reality many people are dealing with and often would rather not speak about. Does it make you feel disloyal or unappreciative to your boss or company? I can understand that rationale, but the advice I'm giving will reassure you otherwise. You may know you're doing nothing more than tolerating your current job, but that doesn't mean you must fail or fall short. You can still perform well while buying time to lay the groundwork for your future endeavor, but a strategic and intentional approach is critically important.

The reality is if you're still with a particular company, whether by choice or not, you owe it them to maintain a high-quality work ethic and do a great job. It may be in your best interests, however, to eliminate extra activities associated with your job. There's a fine balance between doing your job well and going above and beyond when not necessarily required. If you have the authority to delegate, make sure you do so effectively, but by all means, always **inspect what you expect**. This will prevent being blindsided after the fact if tasks aren't performed as anticipated. The last thing you want is to lose your job while you're putting the final touches in place for your transition. I'm not suggesting that you shirk your responsibilities, but don't volunteer for the extras when that time and energy would be better spent preparing for your job change.

I've also learned that you don't have to win every argument and it's not beneficial to buck the system. There's something to be said for following the rules and flying under the radar. Obviously, when you're working in the career of your dreams, you aren't going to want to settle for that approach, but when in a holding pattern, seeking the path of least resistance can be the best route to go. If a situation absolutely requires attention, take your concerns to leadership. Voice them once and then leave the responsibility for corrective actions to management. This way you've done your part, you've made the powers-that-be aware of the situation, but you've absolved yourself from liability. Remember, you don't want to burn any bridges, for your own self-respect or otherwise, and a positive reference is always a plus. Even if you're pursuing a job in an unrelated industry, it never hurts to have solid references, so don't hurt your chances of having them.

Put a smile on your face when you walk in the office door in the morning and make sure it stays there all day. It'll be easier than you think since you'll have the assurance your situation will be changing and each day is getting you closer to realizing your dream. There is hope for your future. You need to save your positive drive and emotions for your true passion, but you must also save your current job while you need it. Don't forget prayer! I had many parking lot prayer moments before going in to work, and they often saved my day.

You may experience guilt in meeting the expectations of your job but not going above and beyond. I understand this as I generally don't do anything if I'm not prepared to give 120%. I want to reassure you, just as I've reassured myself, it's not selfish, unprofessional, or in bad character to perform at standard. You may not get a promotion or raise, but if you're leaving soon, obviously you aren't looking for one. Overachievers, people-pleasers, and hard workers will empathize with the internal pressure we place on ourselves. If you're meeting your employer's standards, keeping your nose clean, and conveying a positive attitude, you're fulfilling your responsibility; this isn't selling your employer short. Sometimes the extra you have to give is best spent on your own personal journey and, if you're following the will of God for your life, this isn't something to be ashamed of.

What starts here? STRATEGIC AND INTENTIONAL PERFORMANCE starts here.

Stay the Course

Every circumstance is different. You may be in a spot where you are waiting to make a change but aren't necessarily hating life or feeling that you're just tolerating your job environment. For me [Sherry] this speaks to where I am. My current job is a good one. I've worked for my cousin, Jeff, and his partner Marty for years, and I do mean years. About 16 of them! Before that, Jeff worked for the business I used to own, so we've got a long history together. I'm the office manager for their floor covering store. I enjoy what I do and am proficient at it. After all this time, I'd better be! "The Bossmen," as I affectionately call them, have allowed me to change my schedule and responsibilities as needed throughout the years. I may not have been able to make every field trip or school event for my sons, but as far as single moms go, I had a good batting average. My job is close to home, hours are flexible, and a casual dress code is strictly enforced. I've always been fairly compensated and received generous benefits and perks. My job has served its purpose and served it well, but things are different now. I have a new mission and passion, and am carving out a new direction with Lindon. While I'm shifting gears, though, I remain extraordinarily grateful and appreciative for my job. I'll continue to give my all until the day I leave. Yes, my focus has definitely changed, but I'm going to do my level best never to let the Bossmen and my co-workers know it.

What starts here? MAINTAINING YOUR FOCUS starts here.

Working the Skills

Whether you are in a job you love or are making plans to leave, chances are a good dose of workplace decluttering is in order. We're going to apply decluttering bits and pieces from previous chapters to your place of business and help you tidy things up on the job scene.

For starters, do you have a work area or an office you call home? Do you drive a vehicle that's synonymous with your office on wheels? Keep your physical space decluttered and free from the excess and unnecessary. Use the principles we discussed in Chapter 1 to help transform your work environment into a place you enjoy being in. Simple tasks like sorting through old papers and shredding them, wiping the coffee and food off your desk or keyboard, vacuuming your floor, or even cleaning off the dash and passenger seat in your vehicle can prevent your work space from suffocating you. Messiness and disorganization will slowly encroach on your ability to work efficiently. Take time out of your busy day to manage your area; it's amazing what a lift a little cleaning brings, especially if your space is limited. Organized, simple, and fresh will allow you to concentrate better and increase your productivity.

I [*Sherry*] was going on vacation but took the time to clean my office from top to bottom before I left. When I returned, I forgot that I'd done this and had quite a surprise waiting for me. It was as if someone spoiled me rotten and left me a gift of epic proportion. An organized desk, sanitized phone, dust-free cubbies, and clean carpet—it was nothing short of amazing. The funny thing was that I could easily experience such pleasure all the time if I simply made the effort to keep my office clean. Reality check!

Next, evaluate your relationships with your co-workers. This is an area where most of us can stand some serious decluttering. Do you get involved with unnecessary conversation which is unproductive at best and often hurtful? Is time spent sharing gossip that is better left out of the workplace? Heck, any gossip at all should be abandoned! Are there competitive or jealous type games being played? Is there unhealthy vying for position or attention? Even the best-intentioned "counseling" has no place in the work arena. If any of these apply, or other similarly destructive situations are present, recognize them for what they are. These are career-altering, life-cluttering, and health-compromising scenarios which must be curbed.

Are you the instigator and offender, or are you on the receiving end of such behavior? Perhaps it's a little of both? Identify the problem, accept your responsibility in rectifying it, and then implement the solution. Attitude adjustments aren't particularly pleasant, but it's definitely easier if it's *your* attitude that needs adjusting. We don't have power or control over how others behave, but we can control ourselves if we're inclined to do so. Do your best to avoid any behavior that isn't beneficial to the company or yourself. Rise above petty conflict and morale-destroying actions. We've all experienced times when it's gratifying to "give someone what they deserve" or one-up an aggravating co-worker who's surely "asking for it," but take heed. Nothing good can come from this type of behavior. Be mindful of God's instruction: "But I tell you that anyone who is angry with his brother will be subject to judgment. Again, anyone who says to his brother, 'Raca', is answerable to the Sanhedrin. But anyone who says, 'You fool!' will be in danger of the fire of hell" (Mt. 5:22).

Yes, while it's often easier said than done to rise above what our emotions are driving us to do, it's not impossible. In light of God's directive on this, it seems a good idea to make your best effort.

If others are the initiators of the conflict, do all you can to promptly remove yourself from the situation. Do not engage! Don't even step into the ring! Surviving harassment isn't easy, but keep your nose clean, do your job to the absolute best of your ability, see past the persecution, and look ahead to the bigger picture. Extreme situations may require the assistance of management to resolve, and if that's the case, don't hesitate to reach out for help. Barring the extreme circumstance, however, just do your best to steer clear of the problems. God gives us great insight on how we should navigate through this type of dilemma: "Blessed are you when people insult you, persecute you and falsely say all kinds of evil against you because of me. Rejoice and be glad, because great is your reward in heaven, for in the same way they persecuted the prophets who were before you" (Mt. 5:11-12).

The key is not to focus on why you're being persecuted because, regardless of the cause, God says the reaction should be the same. This is a tall order when we feel unjustly targeted, isn't it? Can you rejoice and be glad in spite of hurtful treatment? We're still working on perfecting this, but we've each made significant progress and are headed in the right direction. Pick and choose your battles.

You'll be your best at work if you keep your space and relationships as clutter-free as possible, focus on the tasks at hand, maintain a stellar work ethic, and keep yourself free from negativity and drama. Most people spend more time at their jobs than they do with their families or enjoying free time, so it just makes sense to get it right. Use this logic as motivation to make your workplace the most healthy, enjoyable environment possible. You may never get to the point where you're just thrilled to hop out of bed and run into work, but we pray you see there is much you can do to maximize the potential for this to happen.

What starts here? Your CURRENT WORKPLACE DECLUTTERING starts here!

Yours for the Asking

Is it becoming more apparent how these decluttering theme and strategies spill over from one area in your life to another? Principles you've learned about decluttering your finances, home, and relationships are easily applied to your career and work environment. This repetition will make you a pro in no time, and decluttering will come as naturally as cluttering used to.

The pattern being woven throughout *Declutter Now!* continues in this chapter. Putting the brakes on the unimportant leaves more open road for the important. The suggestions we give are just a sampling of what can "start" when you give yourself room and freedom. It's never too late to make adjustments that will positively impact your life, so whatever your situation, do the hard work now and start reaping the benefits for tomorrow.

Stop the "buck" here, and take responsibility for starting whatever will improve the quality of your career and work life. Stop the "dollar" here, and reprioritize the place money has in your life.

"Money never made a man happy yet, nor will it. The more a man has, the more he wants. Instead of filling a vacuum, it makes one." Wise words from Benjamin Franklin.

You may not have felt there were choices in your work life or environment, but we pray that the insight we've shared has gotten your wheels spinning and will be a catalyst for thinking outside the box you feel stuck in. Think big, think progressive, and bring your "A" game. It's yours for the asking.

Chapter 5

Temple Care and Maintenance

DECLUTTERING IS ABOUT TO TAKE on a whole new twist! Throughout the Bible, God comprehensively instructs on anything and everything you need to successfully live your life and serve him. How he wants you to care for your body, your temple, is no exception. While God may not suggest specific veggies to eat, nor does he say how many reps to do when weightlifting, he does take the time to address your physical body in a different sense. Through this discourse, God not only shares his deep love for you and how important you truly are to him, but also issues a direct statement regarding the obligation you have to him for the gift of life he's given you. God abundantly blesses with love, protection, and the assurance of salvation, but in all respects, you should heed your duty to him and take what you've received seriously.

What in the world does a "temple" have to do with your body and why might it need decluttering? What charge do you have in accomplishing this? Why does this matter to God? Take a close look at 1 Corinthians 6:19-20:

"Do you not know that your body is a temple of the
Holy Spirit, who is in you, whom you have received
from God? You are not your own; you were bought at
a price. Therefore honor God with your body."

So, what is a temple? The most common definition is a building or dwelling place devoted to the worship of a god, a place for religious practice. When Paul made this statement in First Corinthians, he was signifying your body is a place where God dwells. He is within you and your body houses and embodies him. How awesome is this? God thinks enough of his children to allow each of our bodies to be a dwelling place for him, the almighty Lord and Creator. The fact he would want to reside within you is a strong statement which exemplifies the love and respect he feels for you, and the importance he places on your relationship with him.

"[W]hom you have received from God…" Not only does God dwell within you and your body is a temple for him, but he is the one solely responsible for giving you your body in the first place. Without him, you would not exist.

"You are not your own; you were bought at a price." God may have given your body to you but it wasn't free. He paid a hefty price; Christ shed his blood to pay that bill. This payment on your behalf obligates you to him. When you occupy something owned by someone else, you have a responsibility to take extra good care of it. It's not just yours to do what you want with at your own discretion. Often, if you're anything like us, you go above and beyond to make sure you keep it in pristine shape. You show your gratitude for your gift by appreciating and caring for it to the best of your ability.

"Therefore honor God with your body." Simply put, when you take care of your body, you are honoring God and being obedient to what he calls you to do. It may seem a bit odd to think of honoring God with your body, but when you break it down and see Paul's wisdom for the truth he preaches, we pray you'll understand that it's anything but odd. When you "honor," you demonstrate respect and high regard. God certainly deserves this reverence, and taking care of the body he entrusted to you is another opportunity to show him your love and gratitude.

When you become a Christian, the Holy Spirit enters you and your body is no longer your own. It's more of a figurative and symbolic entering, but Christ does dwell within you, within your heart, mind, body, and soul. This may seem a little disconcerting at first, but not so much if you remember the Holy Spirit is part of the Trinity; he's one of the good guys! It's not as if some demon-possessed spirit has filled you or you've been taken over by aliens. You made a choice to accept Jesus Christ as your personal Savior, and in doing so, you have the benefit of him entering heart, your life, and your body in the form of the Holy Spirit. This scenario makes a strong argument for why you have a responsibility to take extra special care of your body, doesn't it? This is where decluttering comes in.

Remember, decluttering not only involves removing the negative, but also knowing what is healthy to keep and do. In relation to your body, you must declutter anything which can or does have an adverse effect, and incorporate a healthy lifestyle so you can make maximum use of what you've been given. What exactly does decluttering look like in regard to your physical body? Time to find out!

Just as with any building, your temple needs to have the right components to stand strong and function cooperatively. A building needs footings, plumbing, electrical, heating and air conditioning, paint, flooring, etc., to operate effectively and efficiently as a whole unit. Your temple is much the same, but the components needed and utilized are different. For your physical building, we're going to talk about factors that affect its operation such as drugs, alcohol, prescription medication, sleep, stress, nutrition, and fitness. Some of these you would be wise to incorporate, but others are best to avoid just the same as you would want to avoid faulty wiring and termites in a building.

A myriad of contractors are involved in building a structure. You can tap into that type of expertise through doctors, dieticians, and personal trainers. Before you begin, though, you need to submit plans for approval, and this is just as critical as the work being done well. We pray that our words will encourage you to put your own plan together, a plan to care for and maintain your temple in the way God asks you to. He is, after all, the Master Inspector, so bear this is mind when deciding how earnestly you're going to pursue your upkeep and how much time and effort you're going to invest.

Let us tell you right up front, we're not here to propose a specific weight-loss plan or lay out a detailed exercise routine. That just isn't going to happen! Our goal is to discuss healthy living, including physical, emotional, and spiritual aspects which will encourage you to care for and maintain the body God has entrusted to you. This body is yours for the entire time you spend on earth, and he expects you to take exceptional care of it. It might even help if you don't look at this as a choice; it's your duty. In layman's terms, we've been speaking about how to get the garbage out of our lives, and now it's time to get it out of our bodies! We want you to take this stuff seriously. God does!

NO Question about It!

We'd like to get the obvious out of the way first. Drinking to excess and drug abuse, prescription or otherwise, are absolute "No's." If you have a problem in any of these areas, make no compromise about decluttering them from your life and doing it now! These behaviors, whether willful choices or the result of a chemical dependency or addiction, can be extremely hard habits to break. Some people make a decision to quit cold turkey and do just that, but many can't, even if the desire is there. If you're dependent on drugs or alcohol to any degree, or if you're caving to a craving you wish to curb, please don't hesitate to seek help.

Just for the sake of discussion, and possibly argument, when it comes to drinking, what is excessive? For some who don't partake, one drink is one drink too many. Others enjoy a glass of wine or two and find that perfectly acceptable. We aren't here to set your guidelines or be your moral compass, but we'd like to share God's word on the matter. The Bible has quite a bit to say on the subject of wine. Nowhere in the Word does it indicate that drinking wine is a sin and strictly forbidden. It seems there's a distinction between having a drink and getting drunk. In 1 Timothy 5:23, Paul suggested that Timothy stop drinking water and drink a little wine in an effort to cure his stomach ailments. We wonder if this worked. Clearly wine was not forbidden or Paul wouldn't have encouraged Timothy to sin. Losing control of your senses, as in the case of drunkenness, is where God seems to draw the line. When someone is high on drugs or drunk on alcohol, they're operating and living under the control of those influences. God expects us to live under the influence of the Holy Spirit, not harmful substances. "Do not get drunk on wine, which leads to debauchery. Instead, be filled with the Spirit" (Eph. 5:18).

I [*Sherry*] have a story that illustrates what we're talking about. I used to babysit for a young girl whose father was the pastor at a local Lutheran church. My impression of the pastor was that while he was nice enough, he seemed quite conservative and straight-laced. One Monday afternoon when he was picking his daughter up, he asked her, "What's tonight honey?" and she replied with glee, "Monday Night Football, Daddy!" The Pastor then asked, "And who are you?" To which his daughter enthusiastically responded, "The Beer Meister!"

The beer what? Really? A five-year-old beer *meister*? I was seriously confused and surprised, so I asked the pastor what all this meant. The pastor explained that when watching football on Monday nights, he enjoys a beer; sometimes two. His daughter delights in getting him his beverage while he relaxes in front of the television. As he was sharing, he must have noticed the quizzical look on my face, so he proceeded to explain to me the difference between having a drink and getting drunk. I still must have looked unconvinced or like I was in a state of shock, because the next day he brought me a printout of all the Bible verses which supported his viewpoint. It was interesting and incredibly eye-opening. He wasn't trying to win me over to his point of view, although I wasn't necessarily opposed. I was just in disbelief this somewhat stuffy (SORRY!) pastor enjoyed a beer now and then and had no problem with his young daughter knowing this and physically bringing it to him.

The point of this isn't to encourage you to drink, rationalize its acceptance, or inspire you to turn your child into a beer *meister*. It's merely to share with you what I've learned on my journey and arm you with some basic knowledge so you have a springboard to do your own research and form your own opinion. For the sake of good measure, let's check out the flip side; drinking to excess.

Look at the examples of drunkenness in the Bible. Genesis 9:20 speaks of Noah getting drunk from wine and then being seen in his nakedness by his sons. Not a great witness from this hero of faith. What about Lot? In Genesis 19:32, Lot's daughters got him drunk because they knew it was the only way he would sin in the manner they wanted him to. Drunkenness dulls the senses, causes poor judgment, and will clutter your life with problems and drama. It's between you and God what's acceptable and how much is too much. Lean on his Word and respect his desires when making your choices.

The discussion on drug usage is more clear-cut. Common sense dictates something illegal is wrong and off limits. There's no excuse legitimate enough to warrant ingesting, smoking, or otherwise delivering illicit drugs into your system. The debate on medical marijuana has certainly brought some compelling deliberation to the forefront, but again, we deflect to the legal vs. illegal aspect. Follow the rules. The same applies to prescription drugs. Be honest with your health care provider, only take what's yours, and take the amount prescribed. How many addictions and deaths could be avoided if the rules were just followed?

We would be remiss if we didn't share another concern which weighs heavily on our hearts. Just because a doctor has written a prescription for you, doesn't mean you need it and doesn't mean you should take it. We wholeheartedly concur there are times when medication is necessary and helpful, no question about it. However, that being said, we're also under the impression there are many instances where medication is prescribed too freely, taken without question, and is altogether unnecessary. No offense meant to the responsible doctors whom are plentiful and deeply valued, but as with every profession, there are those who are irresponsible as well.

Last year, Lindon was given a prescription for blood pressure medicine. His blood pressure read high for three visits in a row to the same doctor, in the same examining room, using the same equipment. The odd thing, though, was everywhere else Lindon had his pressure read, such as in other doctor's offices and freestanding machines, it always came back normal. In fact, it had never been even remotely high, except for the three instances in this particular doctor's office. Lindon shared this with the doctor and, without any further questions, discussion, or investigation, the doctor still wrote him the script for blood pressure medicine. Needless to say, Lindon hasn't filled it and instead opted to keep a close eye on his pressure for now. He had it read just days after his last doctor's appointment and, again, it was perfectly normal. Perhaps the equipment is incorrectly calibrated or maybe Lindon experiences anxiety when going to that particular doctor. The latter is unlikely, though, because his pressure is normal even when going to a different doctor for epidural injections in his back. One would suspect if his pressure was going to spike, anticipating an injection in his back would be the perfect instigator.

We're not sure exactly what's going on, but we know one thing for certain. Based on the information at hand, it seems premature to relegate Lindon to a lifelong course of blood pressure medication which he may not even need. We both agree that a longer track record and more information are warranted before he takes such a serious step. We aren't anti-medication, but every medication on the market can have side effects, and some have highly addictive qualities. There's a time and place when it's necessary and beneficial, even life-saving, however, make sure you're at least reasonably convinced it's necessary before agreeing to anything.

We also fear society has come to rely on a pill to fix everything. People seem less inclined to work and would rather just take a magic pill to make everything all better. One pill leads to two, and when that isn't cutting it, the ante is exponentially upped. Yes, you have to rely on your health care providers for sage advice and guidance, but you also have a responsibility to be your own best patient advocate. You must look out for what's right for yourself first and, if you're uncertain, don't hesitate to get a second or third opinion. No blind faith here. Your temple is far too important for shortcuts.

If you find yourself suffering from any type of dependency, there are a wide variety of support groups and programs available which cater to addictions. You can locate programs through your health care provider, church, or community service groups. If you need help, enlist the assistance of family, friends, or clergy. Help is available for the asking and we are imploring you, if you need it, or even are simply concerned you might, pursue getting it without fail. Bring it to God in prayer and ask for guidance and direction. Don't be ashamed of whatever you may be going through. Not obtaining the aid you need and compromising your health and wellbeing is far more embarrassing, not to mention detrimental, than reaching out and attempting to rectify the problem.

A Sleeper of Importance

What else, beyond the obvious, should you avoid? Sleep is a huge factor in your overall healthcare and allowing yourself to become run down and fatigued will trigger a wide-ranging negative domino effect. When your body is compromised, the flood gates swing wide open for a host of problems. Reduced immunity and sickness lead the concerns, with impaired judgment and poor decision-making not far behind. Often productivity at work will suffer, appointments will be missed, classes slept through, and conversations will lack clarity and depth. The need for sleep touches every area of your being.

[*Sherry*] In 2010, my son Devin went through a particularly difficult time. He drove a high performance sports car and spent most of his free time hanging out with the "car guys." To put it mildly, Devin is a bit of an adrenaline junkie and has an insatiable need for speed. The combination of his passion and that environment almost proved deadly. He was in a rollover accident, and only by the grace of God was his life spared. Devin spent several months spinning out of control. He made poor life choices, left home, had no job, and was spiraling. We were terrified. After four long months and a few steps he took in the right direction, we felt it was the right time to ask Devin to come home. He gladly accepted. Devin secured a steady job, curbed his former habits, and started going to his counselor, Jason, for help in sorting things out.

Let me preface the following by saying that nothing fazes Jason. This isn't to say he doesn't care and isn't helpful, but it takes a lot to get a rise out of him. I went with Devin to his first appointment to make sure Jason had a comprehensive snapshot of what had been going on in Dev's life. I felt my perspective would help round out the full story. Jason listened to almost an hour's worth of serious concerns and frightening incidents which were the fabric of Devin's recent past. His posture didn't change at all during that time. It wasn't until the end of our session when I mentioned Devin wasn't sleeping well, in fact, hardly at all, did we get a raised eyebrow and a string of serious questions culminating in a call for immediate action. I explained to Jason that if Devin got two hours of sleep at a time, it was a long stretch. He was often up until at least 3 a.m.

and then would sleep sporadically for the next several hours, waking to answer texts or calls on his phone every few minutes. Devin alluded to the darkness of night bringing out his anxieties and fears, so sleep came at a premium. I didn't know how he was even functioning and, the truth was, he wasn't.

Jason expressed his deep concern over Devin's lack of sleep and educated us on the ramifications of sleep deprivation. I must tell you it was highly alarming for me, as a parent, to see how serious Jason believed the situation to be. I knew sleep was important, but within the mix of all my other concerns, I didn't realize how high in the pecking order this rated. I came to understand this was the underlying cause of a multitude of problems and bad decisions. Jason made it crystal clear that we needed to rectify the problem ASAP.

The following week, Devin went to a doctor to discuss sleeping medication. The idea was to utilize medication to establish a normal sleep pattern and then slowly wean off of it. Since Devin was already in counseling and making positive behavior changes, we hoped by the time he was ready to part with the medication, he would be further along in his progress and able to manage a normal schedule on his own. While we now understood just how important sleep would be, it was still disturbing when we received the exact same concerned reaction from this doctor as we had from Jason.

After giving the doctor the whole ball of ugly wax, he stopped typing notes and looked at Devin. In spite of all the different concerns and problems we shared in an effort to get the doctor up to speed, the first and only area he addressed and lectured Devin on was the importance of sleep to our bodies. He could have mentioned the illegal street racing first, or perhaps the destructive social choices Devin had made, but he didn't. He zeroed right in on Devin's sleep disorder and advised that so many of Devin's problems would either disappear or become far more manageable if his body was getting the required amount of uninterrupted sleep each night. The doctor said the ill effects he observes from sleep-deprived patients are so far reaching, it's one of the single most critical concerns he has when providing care. It's the root cause for a variety of problems.

I've made a big deal about this because it is a big deal, and I really want to drive the point home. Out of all the ways you care for your body, this may be one of the easiest to improve. Once you recognize a problem and understand its severity, it's often not terribly difficult to fix. From all I've experienced and learned, getting enough solid sleep is one of the single most important ways you can care for your temple. Make sure your body is getting the rest it deserves!

Stress Is Distress

STRESS! While you may not have known precisely how important sleep is, most people will readily acknowledge that stress can cause serious health implications. News reports, magazine articles, and brochures in physicians' offices are full of statistics which leave no room for doubt. There is almost no health-related area more important to declutter than this one.

According to Merriam-Webster's dictionary, stress is a physical, chemical, or emotional factor that causes bodily or mental tension and may be a factor in disease causation. If Webster says stress can cause bodily tension or disease, then it must be true! It may be hard to understand how an emotional state can cause a physical problem, but it can and it does, all the time. Here are some statistics:

- 43% of all adults suffer adverse health effects from stress
- 75-90% of all physician office visits are for stress-related ailments and complaints
- Stress is linked to the six leading causes of death: heart disease, cancer, lung ailments, accidents, cirrhosis of the liver, and suicide.
- Behavioral symptoms of stress can include but are not limited to: obesity and over-eating, increased or excessive drinking of alcohol, increased smoking, increased caffeine / coffee consumption, and substance abuse.
- Common physical symptoms of stress and anxiety can include but are not limited to:

  Migraine headaches

  Indigestion

  Nausea

  Heartburn

  Constipation or diarrhea

  Stomach cramps

  Tremors and shaking / nervous twitches

  Muscle cramps / spasms

  Rheumatoid arthritis

  Eczema / psoriasis

  Asthma attacks

  Hair loss

  Neck & back pain

  Chest pain or palpitations

What frightening statistics! Need we continue? This list should be enough to scare anyone. There's enough that can go wrong with your body without your help. Through no fault of your own, diseases or medical conditions can show up at any time, so keep the ones at bay that you have control over. Send stress packing and declutter it forever!

Jesus said, "Who of you by worrying can add a single hour to his life?" (Mt. 6:27). Actually, we'll add that not only does worrying not add any time to your life but, quite literally, it can cut your life short.

Stress can be tricky to manage or rein in. We've each battled our own stressful situations and the consequences from such. Years ago Lindon ended up in the hospital thinking he was having a heart attack only to be told, after extensive testing, that his discomfort was a physical reaction to stress. In the past, Sherry suffered from anxiety and panic attacks which led to many sleepless nights, waking up with the shakes and breaking out in cold sweats. It was no fun at all.

Although stress can get the best of each of us from time to time, God designed us and knows the limits within our human nature. He calls us to seek him out and enlist his help!

"Do not be anxious about anything, but in everything, by prayer and petition, with thanksgiving, present your requests to God" (Phil. 4:6). That's pretty straightforward!

"Come to me, all you who are weary and burdened, and I will give you rest. Take my yoke upon you and learn from me, for I am gentle and humble in heart, and you will find rest for your souls. For my yoke is easy and my burden is light" (Mt. 11:28-30).

How can you possibly resist Jesus' personal invitation? Why would you want to? Cast your problems, your stress, and anxieties on him, and he'll bear the burden of them. You don't have to do this alone; he's there to lighten your load, any time, any place.

If stress is your constant companion, we pray you'll get it under control. Seek God and follow his direction for whatever steps he's leading you to take. Ask your doctor for advice, visit a counselor, research credible self-help material, or find an appropriate support group. Learn how to manage your stress before it wrecks your temple and causes serious cracks in your foundation which can't be easily repaired.

And speaking of foundations, just as with a building, our temple must be built on solid ground, with grade 'A' material and expert labor to best withstand the storms of life. We can't prevent all ailments, but if we do our part and take the best possible care of our bodies, we're giving them a fighting chance of holding up and battling the catastrophes that may come our way. The food we ingest and the exercise we partake in are the two primary sources for laying a strong foundation.

Foundations for Healthy Living

We said at the beginning of this chapter we weren't going to propose a weight-loss plan or lay out an exercise routine. What we are going to do, however, is discuss the benefits of eating healthy and exercising regularly in the hope that if you aren't doing so already, you will be inclined to start both.

Admittedly, it's difficult nowadays to know exactly what to eat. One day there will be an article touting a particular food which has been proven to be detrimental to your health, and the next day a news segment on the benefits of that same food will be on your local 5 p.m. news. Some nutritionists promote watching your carbs while others primarily focus on caloric intake. Depending on your individual dietary needs, allergies or health conditions, there may be a host of foods to avoid and others you would benefit from incorporating into your daily routine. What to do and how to declutter the confusing mess of information being tossed your way from every direction can be overwhelming.

Our recommendation is to keep it simple and start with the sure bets. Fruits and vegetables generally don't garner too much controversy in the health world, but where do you go from there? We try to avoid a lot of the white stuff (sugar, bread, rice, and pasta), go light on butters, and avoid heavy creams. We enjoy chicken, seafood in moderation, meat occasionally, and healthy (most of the time!) snacks between meals. And if we have dessert, it's frozen yogurt or light popcorn.

Not only should you be careful of the choices you make for the food you eat but, to make a noticeable difference in how you feel, you need to declutter the unhealthy foods from your diet. What indulgences should you curb or cut out? Figure out how to manage your weaknesses and avoid bingeing on the harmful. Make no mistake about it; we love chips, french fries, chocolate, pizza, and hot wings (though not necessarily all at the same time). But our resolve is to keep these splurges to a minimum.

Exercise is a priority for us. We don't belong to a gym but prefer working out at home, walking, hiking, and swimming. When the weather is conducive, we try to get moving at least five nights per week and walk two to five miles. Even in the brutal Arizona summer, we're out walking at least two to three nights per week and then exercise in the pool to make up for the slack. Ahhhh, it's a rough life!

The eating and exercise regimen we've established works for us, but we aren't going to win any "Hot Body" contests, that's for sure, nor are we examples of the perfect, organic-only eating specimens. We're content with the health and fitness level that our routine affords and enjoy the wiggle room we allow ourselves. It's a happy medium.

This may or may not be close to your desires or needs, but we're not here to tell you exactly what to do. We are just hopeful that we'll motivate you to do something!

Couple responsible eating with daily exercise and you've exponentially increased your odds for living a healthier life. Studies show walking just thirty minutes each day can provide huge heart benefits, and every one hour of walking may increase your life expectancy by two hours. Those are far better odds than most things we gamble on! Check out the American Heart Association's website, www.heart. org., for a great place to start gathering information on how nutrition, physical activity, weight management, stress management, and quitting smoking all play lead roles in getting and staying healthy.

When it comes to your activity regimen, be intentional and consistent in your exercise so you can reach and maintain the fitness level you desire. Turn your expensive, oversized clothes hanger, a.k.a. treadmill or weight bench, back into a piece of workout apparatus and get going! Yes, it takes effort and time to accomplish this, but as you declutter the unnecessary from your life, you'll naturally have more time for the activities which are clear priorities, and becoming healthier most assuredly rates right up there! You must take responsibility for your physical wellbeing, and we pray you energetically pursue making your goals a reality.

You Can Do It!

"I can do everything through him who gives me strength" (Phil. 4:13). "Him," of course, is Christ Jesus. Whatever crosses you bear, all things are possible if you seek your ability from Jesus.

In search of inspiration? Consider the individual, hundreds of pounds heavier than you, who is committed to taking the weight off one pound at a time, and always has a smile. Think about people with severe impairments or handicaps who continue to grind through grueling workouts with an undeniable spirit of hope and determination. Stories abound of people with incredible willpower and optimism.

We have a neighbor we see walking most nights we're out. We've befriended him and have had the extreme pleasure of getting to know him. He's had five back surgeries, with one more to go, and is in pain for the better part of each day of his life. He doesn't have much in the way of reprieve from the agony, yet he walks three miles EVERY SINGLE NIGHT with his trusty beagle Buster by his side. He even does this in the summer's blistering evening heat, taking more frequent breaks than in cooler months just to make it through his workout. When we stop to chat, he is sweating profusely and clearly uncomfortable, often leaning on a fire hydrant or electrical box to give his aching back a quick break. Whenever we get lazy or feel sorry for ourselves, we think of our neighbor and what an amazing inspiration he is. No one is forcing him out the door each night, and he's well aware that his best day is worse than anything most people will experience. You may have constraints to work within (our neighbor isn't going to run a 10K anytime soon), but stop making excuses and put your best foot forward, literally.

[*Lindon*] I have had my share of struggles with back pain, which were exacerbated by weight gain and emotional stressors. The impact on my physical wellbeing was challenge enough, but the toll taken on my emotional health only caused me to further spiral, which in turn, delayed my physical healing. It was not a progressive cycle to say the least.

In 2003, I suffered a torn L5 disc, causing heavy pressure on my sciatic nerves, as well as on nerves leading away from the area which supplied my stomach and digestive tract. I suffered unbearable pain that rendered me immobile and feeling as if I could not breathe. I endured many ambulance rides to the ER, heavy doses of pain-killing medications, and numerous epidural treatments, all of which didn't solve the problem. The initial injury landed me in decompression with a *clamshell vest*, not an attractive image, especially since I looked swollen from the extra weight I'd gained. The additional pounds, of course, added to my discomfort. I had no income and needed to formulate a new game plan for a future career. It was tough accepting that my career as an audio-visual guy was over, and this bred tremendous stress. The stress, of course, brought more physical problems. Add to the mix a marriage going down the drain, and you'll begin to understand how devastating this perfect storm was. I spent several months lying on my back, watching daytime talk TV, feeling sorry for myself, and eating. Miserable doesn't begin to describe my physical and mental state.

During this time, though, I was blessed with learning to fully rely on God. Through "miracles in the mailbox," I was cared for with food left on my doorstep, financial surprises, and the support of friends and strangers alike. I had no choice but to trust God, and I'm thankful I knew him during this period of my life. I can't imagine undergoing such a trying time without the reassurance of knowing he was there with me.

Gradually my back began healing. Tom, a member of my church who was a stranger to me at the time, approached me in the parking lot, mentioned a job opening, and asked if I was interested. A miracle! Heck yeah I was interested! I got the job and the slow, uphill climb began, but my trials weren't over. The next few years brought more job changes, back issues that continually reared up, and a marriage which finally completely fell apart. It dawned on me that while I knew God, I wasn't living in close communion with him, and I had no motivation to serve. Instead I was walking down the path of "I can fix all this, I am in control, and I can handle these losses." *I, I, I!* The problem was the "I." (There is no "I" in God.) I was confronted with the realization I wasn't leaning on the Lord to help guide and direct me through these stressful, crushing times. I was aware of and grateful for his presence, but I wasn't trusting him or being completely obedient.

I started walking and talking to God, all the while praying for his healing and intervention in my life. There was a mountain just west of my home and every day I'd slowly and arduously walk three to five miles around the base of the mountain. I prayed. I cried. I whined and complained to God about all that had happened and all I was losing. While I knew in my heart the marriage was over long ago, I still felt unjustly wronged. There was so much to walk and think through, but always present was the hope that things were going to get better. After each walk, I would go to a park bench, watch the sun go down behind the mountain, and think I was another day closer to arriving at where God wanted me to be. I gave it all up to him, prayed unceasingly, and begged him not to let me end up with a hard heart. I knew anger, bitterness, and sadness was raging within me, and I was deeply scared. Still, nothing seemed to change.

As anticipated, I eventually received an eviction notice and was forced to leave my home. My daughter had already moved out with her mother, but my son decided to stay with me. We took an apartment close to where I was working and lived without TV, cable, or internet. We barely had any furniture. It was a modest existence, to put it mildly, but there was still room for things to get worse. Sounds like the theme from the most depressing movie ever, doesn't it? I was hit with several large, unexpected bills and the tax man was forever knocking at my door. As it was, I could barely pay my rent and expenses and sometimes, in moments of weakness, I wondered if things were ever going to change for the better. Deep in my heart, though, I still believed I was one day away from a major breakthrough, from a miracle changing my life.

I went to church sporadically and began ministering to neighbors I met at the pool in the apartment complex where I lived. I started praying for people poolside, and even did a few impromptu Bible studies there. It wasn't much, but I was attempting to serve God in some capacity, and it felt pretty good. It felt good to feed myself as well. I was in my apartment just four months when I met Sherry. That is when everything began to drastically improve!

Through miracle after miracle, every part of my life came together. I landed a new job with a large pay increase, debts were reduced and then paid off, and bonuses were bigger than anticipated. Sherry found out my insurance covered a spinal decompression treatment which was life changing. We started going to church together regularly and began serving, first as greeters, then helping with audio, and now as small group leaders. I began laying the foundation for the men's ministry I was passionate about and had been formulating in my head for years. I even lost the weight I needed to lose. In time, I came to understand that God had a different plan for my life than what I had imagined, and somehow I had to "Let Go, Let God." I used to hear that saying and while catchy, it didn't resonate until then. It was no more just "I."

It was a long road, about six years long. The initial disc injury wasn't something I signed up for, but through my experiences I've learned much about making the right choices in caring for my temple, and how important a positive path to healing is. I'm keenly aware how this directly impacts not only my wellbeing, but my obedience and service to God. Yes, I'm constantly reminded of the limitations with my back, but I've progressed, by his grace, to a place where I have energy, can exercise regularly, and have the freedom, both physically and mentally, to serve. I now understand the correlation between caring for my temple and my responsibility to him, and I strive daily to do the best I can with what I have. When problems recur, as they sometimes do, or when I feel weak in making the right choices for my body, I remind myself of the awesome gift God has given me and why it's my obligation to take care of it.

Investing in Your Success

If you're struggling with a weight problem or have a physical ailment, limitation or need, seek out a doctor, nutritionist, an experienced and qualified weight trainer who would be an asset in helping you build the perfect plan for your health and fitness endeavor. As we mentioned when discussing finances, there's a time to declutter and curtail spending, but there are also legitimate reasons to part with your hard-earned money. If you need to lose a substantial amount of weight, it may cost more money for the food to stick to a specific program, or you may have to incur the expense of having a physical therapist or personal trainer working side by side with you, pushing you every step of the way. We aren't suggesting you throw money away, but if self-discipline is a particular area of weakness, or if you need the expertise of a professional to get you to the next level, you may need to invest a little to gain a lot. Weigh and balance, so to speak!

Buyer Beware

If your struggle is specifically weight control, there are a multitude of diet and workout programs available. Some are good for you, but certainly not all. Many tout instant results and often promise guarantees. Don't be swayed by unrealistic claims and miracle cures. Consult your doctor and get his *permission* before starting any diet or nutrition program, or undertaking an exercise program that's more physically demanding than anything you currently participate in. Ask his advice regarding programs you're considering.

The food we ingest and our physical behaviors influence how much wear and tear we impart on our temple, but done well, these same behaviors can support the building of a solid structure that will endure through the years. Think about the three little pigs in the fairy tale and the kinds of houses they built of straw or sticks or bricks. Different approaches can produce drastically different results. Which one would you want representative of your body?

God's Design

Do you ever question God's design? Why am I so short? Why do my ears stick out? How come I have such thin hair? Why are my eyes so close together? GRRR! The list of possible grievances is endless. Most of us don't look exactly how we'd like to and probably never will. When these moments of self-doubt and criticism creep in, remind yourself the decisions on how you were formed weren't up to you. You were designed exactly as God saw fit. The desire to tuck this and nip that is overwhelming for some. We too have our own personal wish list and struggle with accepting the beauty God has given us. God's standard of perfection, though, is not based on the world, and the sooner you accept this, the quicker you'll find peace. Whose standards would you rather measure up to anyway? God's or the world's? Yes, you have an obligation to take great care of what God has blessed you with, but you aren't called to look like air-brushed, photo-shopped models who don't remotely resemble the real person they are.

[*Sherry*] I was discussing this chapter with a close friend, Angie, and she made an astute observation. She said when at the gym, she sees well-sculpted "temples" everywhere. Gorgeous bodies, tight abs, and muscles of steel. There are those who work out to stay fit and healthy as part of a balanced lifestyle, and there are those who are completely obsessed and fixated with their body image for all the wrong reasons. Angie said as she looked around the gym, it dawned on her that many of the temples are empty tombs—people who look beautiful on the outside but who don't know the love of Christ or have any idea what he has to offer them on the inside. So many gorgeous but lost souls living unfulfilled and hopeless existences. What an unsettling realization, but also what a fitting opportunity to remind ourselves what should be most important.

It's easy to get discouraged or disgusted with your body if you focus on every little dimple or imperfection, but remember, by human nature we are all flawed. Your directive should be to do the best you can with what God has bestowed upon you and check the rest off your list. Praise God for exactly what he's created in you and keep your eyes focused on the splendor of all that makes you unique. Trust in God's design!

Wise Counsel

In Proverbs 4:20-22, Solomon addresses what brings health to your body: "My son, pay attention to what I say; listen closely to my words. Do not let them out of your sight, keep them within your heart; for they are life to those that find them and health to a man's whole body."

Proverbs 4 primarily deals with Solomon's advice in regard to making wise choices. He takes a hard line on the choices we have, which he believes are limited to either the path of the wicked or the path of the righteous; he doesn't see much in between. Take a moment and read this chapter if you're not familiar with it. It's quite short and will only take a minute or so. What great counsel on making good decisions and going after what's right, while not allowing yourself to be swayed by evil and temptations. We particularly enjoyed his link between the words he was speaking and a man's health.

Solomon knew it wasn't his words themselves which would make you healthy but godly wisdom put into practice that would do the trick. He learned at a very young age the most important choice he could make was to seek God's wisdom at all times in all he did. This course of action is the key to obtaining good health and, if you enjoy good health, you are caring for the temple God has given you.

There are certainly a variety of other ways in which you can declutter your body. We hope the suggestions we've provided will change the way you think about the care and maintenance of your temple. Taking care of yourself for your own personal reasons and for the sake of those that love you is purpose enough, but add to the mix the "God Factor" and it should amp up your motivation. The fact that he has made requests of you which directly address your responsibility to him should cause you to take note and step it up a notch.

No Risk, All Gain

We began with a verse in the Bible that speaks to God's position on how we should care for our bodies and why. Let's look past that, for a moment, and touch on some of the other beneficial reasons for decluttering your body.

The premise of decluttering is to allow you the freedom to have choices. The same holds true for this facet of decluttering. If you're fit and healthy, you have the freedom to enjoy a multitude of activities. A healthy lifestyle will never limit you, whereas being unfit may impose restrictions. When people don't have the freedom they'd like, we refer to this as "giving up their power." We're not control freaks, but are strong supporters of ensuring you have the ability to make your own decisions. If you give up your power, then you're simply at the mercy of choices that others make for you or what you obtain by default. You fall into the "you get what you get" scenario. Personally, this doesn't fly for us.

If you take good care of yourself, you'll be in a better position to enjoy your children and increase your chances for sticking around as long as possible. (Even if you elect not to participate in an activity, you'll have the satisfaction of knowing it was by your choice, not because you gave away your power to choose.) Financially, it's a win–win too. You won't be spending loads of money on an addiction, on prescription drugs to manage poor health, or on all the extra food you would have been consuming. When you take good care of yourself, typically your doctors' appointments won't be as frequent and you'll keep yourself out of most high risk groups that no one would willingly opt into. Blood pressure and cholesterol will be lower. You'll have more energy and be less prone to injury and will heal faster if you do get hurt or need surgery. Often, you'll sleep better. Good health even affects your attitude and general sense of wellbeing. The benefits are endless, and as far as we can tell, there are no detrimental side effects in taking great care of your temple.

One last advantage, as with all the other decluttering exercises, is the most important benefit behind the effort. Serving God! How much more effectively can you minister and how much better will your ability be if you're ready to go anywhere, at any time, to do anything? You'd be completely at God's disposal. How wonderful would that be? Can you serve God if you struggle with a weight problem or health issue? Absolutely! It just makes logical sense, though, that the healthier you are, the fewer problems you may encounter which could hold you back. The healthier you are, the more energy you'll have for service. The healthier you are, the better witness you'll be on caring for the temple that God entrusted to you.

Giving Back

"Therefore, I urge you, brothers, in view of God's mercy, to offer your bodies as living sacrifices, holy and pleasing to God—this is your spiritual act of worship" (Rom. 12:1). Isn't this just a beautiful verse? There is a comfort and peace in this beauty. God isn't asking us to read his mind. He's telling us straight up what to do and why we should do it. No guessing games or mind trips. Just simple facts and directives all delivered with a love for us greater than anything our minds can comprehend. We simply have to listen and obey. Care for your temple, folks; it's the only one we get here on earth. Declutter it so you are left with all that is good and pleasing to yourself and to God, and then take that goodness and serve him in a mighty way.

Chapter 6

Our Kids: A Decluttering Work in Progress

[*SHERRY*] **MY SON, DEVIN, ONCE** had a t-shirt that read "Under Construction" on the front. It was one of those "God" shirts with clever Christian slogans. This particular shirt had "Work in Progress" on the back, and each of the letters forming the words were made up of assorted tools—drills, wrenches, hammers, screwdrivers, etc. This struck me as a poignant reminder of our obligation and commitment to our children. God is working on them; he guides, directs, and nurtures. While he's their Heavenly Father and takes great care of our kids, we, as their earthly parents, also have an awesome responsibility to participate in the process of childrearing, right alongside him.

Your kids didn't ask to be conceived. It was by your doing, with a little divine assistance of course, they were brought here, and you owe them. What is owed may vary from each parent's perspective, but most won't deny a newborn baby deserves to be fed, a toddler deserves routine medical care, and an adolescent child deserves an education. That's a miniscule sampling, but it demonstrates your indebtedness to them. Your children will always be your "kids" no matter how old they are and, even with adult children, you may well delight in being part of their lives and enjoy helping when needed. The difference is when these kids become adults, parental help transitions from an obligation to a choice. If you've done your job well and given your children what they deserved and needed as they grew, the level of your assistance will be reduced as responsibility gradually shifts from your shoulders to theirs.

Raising children is not only an obligation of your time and wallet, but also a commitment of your energy, emotions, and love. Most parents want to get it right! You *must* get it right if you want THEM to get it right! It's inevitable, try as you might, there are countless lessons your kids are going to have to learn for themselves and, unfortunately, often learn the hard way. You are charged, however, to lay the groundwork for their success. You must do all you can to ensure they head in the right direction and are equipped with what they'll need to be successful in life. You are given the responsibility of preparing your kids for their future, and the decluttering tools you're gathering in *Declutter Now!* are prime-time material to use in this undertaking.

God urges you to utilize your experiences to instruct your children. He wants you to share with them your successes and failures alike so they can learn from your journey. Joel 1:3 says, "Tell it to your children, and let your children tell it to their children, and their children to the next generation." God calls you to pass along your wisdom and instruction. Maybe they'll listen and learn and maybe they won't but for you, as a child of God, being obedient to his requests is your first priority.

Do you remember the old saying, "Do as I say but not as I do?" Most of us have used that or at least implied it a time or two. It doesn't work well, does it? You can't lead without example! Make no mistake about it. How you manage your own life directly impacts your children's lives and development. It's sobering to think every single thing you do, or don't do for that matter, will have a marked effect in some way on them. It's like you're under a spotlight, and they're watching and taking notes at all times—a bit daunting if you understand the magnitude, but a great reality check to help parents stay the course. Beyond that, you must make an intentional effort to teach and instill what you want passed along to your children. While your kids will glean a few lessons naturally, others will have to be purposefully taught to them.

To be solely accountable for the life of another is a huge responsibility and, if you truly grasp what we're saying, you may feel a new, overwhelming sense of responsibility or conviction for the enormous task at hand. We know we do! But not to worry. Now that the tone is set, we're ready to dig in.

Decluttering with your kids is a two-step process which will first evaluate and define your contribution and then shift into equipping your children. This chapter, while primarily focused on your children, is really just as much about you as it is them. Step by step we'll arm you with sound advice which will get you going in the right direction and keep you there. Are you already headed that way? Wonderful! Then incorporate what we're sharing into your own unique mix and further increase your effectiveness and success.

Let's start at the beginning—the very beginning!

The Exponential Factor

When expectant parents think of their first bundle of joy, they often envision a babe wrapped in swaddling clothes, beautiful rosebud lips, and eyelashes that gently rest on a sleeping face. As experienced parents, such perfection may fleetingly enter our minds, but then we immediately shift to picturing them as little magnifying glasses, perfectly formed convex lenses which will magnify every aspect of our lives in frightening and naked detail. Trust us when we say whatever was before they were arrived, will only be *more so* after they're born, and this refers to the good, the bad, the pretty, and the ugly. Babies can bring tremendous joy into your life and we're not discounting this in the slightest. Just be aware of the flipside. Every challenge you're dealing with will grow exponentially. Each one will be that much more noticeable, irritating, and overwhelming; it's just a fact.

There's so much joy and delight in raising children: the sloppy wet kisses, *squooshable* hugs, heartwarming giggles, amazement in watching their first steps, pride in their accomplishments, and sheer gratefulness for their existence. We're going to speak, however, to some of the less-than-easy moments. We'll tackle potential challenges and tough stuff, as well as offer some preventative maintenance tips and tools which will ward off undesirable behaviors or circumstances.

No Job for Little Johnny

Babies don't fix people or relationships—ever. Never bring children into this world with a "job" already waiting for them! So many people believe that once the baby is born, everything will be okay. If you're starting out behind the eight ball and expecting the baby to fix it all, you're placing an unfair burden on this precious soul who didn't ask to be here in the first place. Don't impose your problems, marital or otherwise, on your baby.

We've known many three-year-olds, who by no fault of their own, could already use counseling and a good dose of decluttering themselves. How ridiculous does this sound? Exactly! Children deserve to begin with a clean, fresh slate, and you owe it to them to do everything in your power to make sure that's what they get. Even with the most ideal start, they will encounter bumps in the road, so begin in the best position possible and give yourself space for detours when the going gets tough.

Have you ever heard a teacher say on the first day of school, everyone starts out with an "A" and it's simply the student's responsibility to keep it? We see it much that way for babies. They're born pure and innocent, not marred or downtrodden by problems and stress, and it's your responsibility to keep them that way, at least initially. They'll make their own mistakes and, yes, real life will happen, but make a commitment to do your best for your children from the get-go and give them the best possible launch.

It's Never Too Late

By your choice and God's design, your little bundle of joy is part of your life. It's your job to deal with your personal challenges before your baby's arrival so his or her innocence won't be met with negativity right out of the chute. But if your baby is already here, don't worry! Even if your angel is now a hairy, grumpy teenager who towers over you, take heart. It's never too late to make positive adjustments. With determination, a solid game plan, and a consistent effort, big changes can happen quite quickly. Human nature tends to become numb to the same ol', same ol', and we often settle for adapting, accepting, denying, ignoring, or tolerating. That produces a total failure to recognize problems, and then we don't stand a chance at repairing them. The key is to mentally step outside the situation so you can objectively recognize the problems and develop an action plan to declutter them.

Assessing the Atmosphere

For starters, ask yourself what your home environment is like? It's easy to feel the atmosphere when you walk into a room. There's a presence of sorts—a mood. Does your home have an air of love, peacefulness, and positive energy permeating throughout, or is there a feeling of darkness, negativity, and tension present? If the latter prevails, you're compromising the unity of your family's foundation by breeding a harmful and destructive situation. Don't allow it to continue. It's the parents' responsibility to remove stress and anxiety from the home, no matter what it takes to accomplish it. Our kids don't have a choice, and they shouldn't have to deal with dissention, emotionally scarring mood swings, and trauma left by chaos. Children shouldn't feel obligated to take sides, be expected to parent the parents, or be privy to conversation suitable only for adults. They should never feel depressed or fearful about coming home or being in the home for any reason!

When we think of destructive home environments, we often envision parents yelling, fighting, and throwing things, but a negatively charged atmosphere isn't just a result of a bad marriage. It can also stem from just one unhappy or stressed-out parent who has problems at work, is worried about a family member going through a rough time, or has a friend on their last nerve breeding nonstop conflict. They may be in the middle of a difficult medical treatment or a nasty divorce. If you recognize yourself in any of these situations, own your responsibility to yourself and your family and resolve whatever is causing you strife. This single directive might call you to a whole lot of hard work, effort, and sacrifice, and you may have to declutter many areas of your life to get the desired end result, but whatever it takes, make it happen because the alternative is far, far worse.

While we didn't have the pleasure of raising kids together, we each experienced similar home environment themes. Our homes had the appearance of happiness. There wasn't yelling and fighting. All of our kids knew they were loved and had the assurance we would go out of our way to provide for them. Below the surface, though, was an abundance of tension in each of our marriages and our homes. We thought our kids were protected from the truth and the fallout which emanates from dissention, but we each found out otherwise later. Kids aren't naïve. They pick up on everything; it goes back to the spotlight and magnifying glass theory! All of the kids have shared, in some way that they were well aware life wasn't as we tried to make it appear. One of our kids even exclaimed "finally!" when being told about the impending divorce. This "child" was saddened by the situation in general but expressed more relief for an end to the pretend life and underlying tones of constant conflict. What a reality check for a parent who thought the kids were none the wiser. We each tried to shield our children, but we obviously weren't as successful as we thought. Both of our negative situations went on far longer than was healthy. We implore you not to wait. Whatever it takes, if it's broken, please fix it! Even if it just needs a little adjustment or fine tuning—get it done!

Let Us Be Clear

We'd like to be clear about something before we continue. When we advise "removing" the negativity and clutter, in the case of marital strife we aren't necessarily advocating for divorce. At times, divorce may be the only answer; no one should be relegated to staying in an abusive or life-threatening situation, but that aside, we are generally first inclined to encourage counseling and aggressively tackling the problems. Perhaps a shift in friendships or social activities is needed? To improve your family time or financial stability, a job or career change might be warranted. Sometimes with a little effort the fix is easy, and sometimes it's not. We can't speak to your exact situation but rather want to impress upon you, either way, to analyze your problems and do whatever it takes to make things better. Professional victims aren't good for much and complaining without seeking resolution, living miserably and, worse, having this affect your children is unconscionable. Don't minimize the importance of the decisions you make and the role you have as your children's mentor and advocate. You MUST walk the talk!

Protecting Our Precious

When you send your children into the world, they'll invariably come under attack from an abundance of forces outside the home. With enough of that to go around, they shouldn't have to deal with negativity *inside* the home as well. Relationships with teachers, peers, co-workers, etc., can and will provide their own share of difficulties. Our kids should feel protected and secure at home. It should be their (and your) place of peace, their refuge and safe haven from the ills and stresses of what they may encounter elsewhere, their place to recharge and rest, and their source for encouragement and shoring up when needed. They should expect an understanding ear, loving hug, and even gentle kick if necessary! Home should be a haven for acceptance and unconditional love. This may sound Pollyannaish but, truly, it isn't an unrealistic expectation if you have the right ideas and effort to match.

While we were writing this section, there was a local breaking news story about a ten-year-old girl, Ame, who had died. Initial reports suggested the chest she was found dead in had been her hiding place during an innocent game of hide and seek. Subsequent reports quickly dismissed this theory. The truth was this little child had been the victim of horrific abuse for most of her life. Ame had been removed from her mother's custody only to be placed with other family members who continued the cycle of abuse. She was tormented and tortured. She slept on the floor of a stall shower with no pillow or blanket because she had a bed wetting problem. Ame had been smeared with feces from time to time and forced to walk on the scalding Arizona summer concrete for punishment. She had to crush cans with her bare feet, was deprived of food, and locked in the chest repeatedly, which ultimately became her death chamber. The chest was airtight and over a foot shorter than she was. Her poor little knees were bruised from the lid slamming down on them. On the night of her death, Ame had been caught "stealing" a popsicle from the refrigerator. She was forced to stay in a back bend position for hours, then told to drag the chest in so her tormentors, her own adult cousins, could force her into it and lock it tight. Her cousins then went to bed. Who knows if they forgot about her or left her there intentionally? But sometime during the early morning this precious young girl, just days shy of her eleventh birthday, died.

We cannot get Ame out of our heads. We are grief-stricken over what she endured emotionally and physically. There are no words to express the pain our hearts feel for her. It's even more dreadful to think the pain we feel doesn't even remotely touch what she suffered. She was failed on so many levels. Ame was abused by the family who should have valued and adored her, ignored by the neighbors who knew what was going on and said nothing, and let down by the system which should have protected her.

This young girl *never* knew true love. She never experienced a home that provided peace and security. She had no idea what compassion, encouragement, or support felt like, and missed out on all the hugs and affection every child should get. It's heartbreaking from start to finish. Seasoned, veteran police officers were rocked to their core and commented it was one of the most horrific cases of child neglect, abuse, and torment they'd ever seen. We can't imagine how she felt, what she endured, or honestly, how she even survived the ten years that she did.

While this is one of the most extreme examples imaginable, it drives the point home. Ame never experienced the type of home or environment we are suggesting should be the norm for every child. Beyond blatant, obvious abuse, it hurts us to even think of kids feeling stressed out over family drama. We don't want them lying awake at night wondering if they could have done something to keep mom and dad from splitting up. Could they have behaved better or helped out more? Children shouldn't have to feel like their parents' caretakers or carry adult burdens on their small shoulders, which happens far too frequently. Age-appropriate responsibilities are one thing, but when your child becomes your mediator, counselor, or confidant, something's wrong. Kids have their own challenges; they don't need yours.

Identifying the Obscure

It's easy to pat yourself on the back. You don't beat your children, withhold food, or prohibit them from going to school. Avoiding the biggies is easy for most of us, but it's the less obvious infractions that slip under our radar all day long. Unfortunately, these have their own devastating consequences. The key is to be aware of your personal areas of weakness and actively guard against playing into them.

Do you ever speak ill of your spouse or ex-spouse? Ask your children to make an uncomfortable phone call because you don't want to?

Lay your burdens at your children's feet or complain about things your kids have no business hearing? Do you snap at them and then apologize, only to snap and then apologize again? Are you always rushing them to do everything faster? Do you hold your children back because of your own fears and insecurities? Are you living vicariously through your kids and pressing them to make decisions you want made, not necessarily encouraging them to make the choices they want or that would be best for them? Are your children subject to being spoken down to or being emotionally abused? Do you sometimes lash out and smack or push them? Do they wake up to arguing and yelling in the home or have to sit through tension-filled dinners night after night where swallowing food past the lump in their throats is impossible? Are you making promises you have no intention of keeping just to pacify them or going back on your word when the going gets tough? Do you miss your children's sporting or school events because of work or because you'd rather be at happy hour with the guys or at the salon getting your nails done? If you answered yes to the last question, all your children know is you're absent. Missing is missing and you're MIA.

This list is harsh. As we read over what we've written, we wonder if we've gone too far. But the huge sense of responsibility we feel to speak our hearts overrides our fears. We know from personal experience that the best of intentions doesn't always equate to the best parenting. No matter how hard we try, we aren't going to achieve perfect parent status. Thank God we aren't called to be perfect because it's not even remotely possible. How much more successful will you be as a parent, and how much happier will your children be if you at least try to right the wrongs? The law of averages is on your side. The more you try, the more you will succeed; some good will have to come out of it. If nothing else, your children will feel more loved by sheer reason of your effort.

It may seem like a stretch to associate parenting with decluttering, but decluttering the negative and destructive is really the first step in having a good foundation to work from with your kids. We know it sounds like a basic notion, but the significance of recognizing and correcting problems cannot be overstated. It's only through this process that lives and futures can be changed forever.

Our Commitment to the DFZ

At age forty-five, we've each experienced years of lessons learned and can now proudly call our home the "Drama Free Zone"! We do our best to approach everything with a positive and loving heart. We're open and honest, talk things through, and leave nothing hanging or to chance. Anyone who isn't willing to support our "zone" standards is welcome, and sometimes even requested, to leave. As with everything, our record isn't flawless, and we don't fool ourselves into thinking it ever will be, but we strive daily to walk our talk. We believe with all our hearts this is what we are called to do and is right in the eyes of the Lord.

The Gift that Keeps on Giving

Let's say your home environment is already a place of harmonious joy and eternal bliss. Ours, on our best day, is certainly not so, but we'll play along with you. Seriously though, your home is in order and there's enough love and goodness to go around. You've got a respectable set of "tools" and are utilizing them to the best of your ability. Things are good, maybe even great. What's next? It's time to shift the focus from getting your personal and home life in order to coaching your kids. You want a clutter-free life to be as second nature for them as putting on a seatbelt when they get in the car. (You DO make them do that, right?)

Because their personalities and ages, needs, interests, and abilities vary, take a custom approach to each child when guiding them. Can you imagine the benefits of teaching your kids to declutter their rooms, hearts, and lives from the beginning so they're forever equipped with the principles for clutter-free living? How much easier for your children to live this way from the start? So much grief could be avoided, not to mention massive decluttering later. What a leg up! What a time *and* heart saver!

You can buy them the latest trendy clothes, the fastest BMX bicycle, or the newest release of a home gaming system CD, but the gift of decluttering will last a lifetime. It will far surpass the momentary excitement of a material present, and while they may not fully comprehend the significance now, they'll thank you over and over again later. Life doesn't have to be so darn hard, and if you can help your kids find more success with less pain, wouldn't you want to? Often this type of gift takes a whole lot more time and energy for the parent as opposed to simply paying for their present at the checkout stand, but realize how much more vital what you're giving them is.

Getting Started

How do you shrink your decluttering tools down to a level your kids can relate to and understand? A perfect starting point is their bedroom. This is their space, their personal territory, their own little part of the world. Kids need to be kids… They need to play, create, and have some room to roam, within boundaries of course. They even need to know it's okay to be messy at times! Establishing a sanitary and antiseptic bedroom isn't the objective. The goal is to encourage order, cleanliness, and a sense of responsibility and pride within them.

[*Sherry*] For instance, I stair-stepped the level of my boys' responsibilities as they grew. When they were just two or three years of age, I had them help me put their undies (forgive me, boys) and socks away in drawers and help with toy clean up. Down the road, they were expected to hang their shirts and pants up and make their beds. The older they got, the more I asked. Eventually, they were cleaning their bathroom and doing their own laundry. Would it have been easier for me to just put their socks away or make their beds in the first place? Oh, yes! But this would have been of no benefit whatsoever to my boys.

Also, consider this. You'll have an easier time soliciting your children's cooperation later if they've been trained to help all along, as opposed to just putting your foot down one day and making demands they aren't accustomed to. If you end up with a fight on your hands each time a request is made, you will be more apt to fall into the "it's just quicker and easier to do it myself" routine and let them off the hook. Don't go there! This may seem like an easier route initially, but you're selling your kids short and preventing them from learning valuable and necessary life skills. We're firm believers that our kids, and people in general, will rise to just about any reasonable expectation, so make sure you aren't the lazy one in the relationship. Don't be the root cause for their failure. Help them help themselves!

The Family Team

Along with whatever personal responsibilities you deem appropriate for your children, there should also be tasks assigned for the common areas of the house. The family is a team and all members should pitch in and feel a stake in how the home is maintained. Impress on your children it has nothing to do with the allowance they may or may not be receiving.

It's about the sense of pride and accomplishment living in a comfortable home brings; it's about having a clean and presentable place in which to entertain friends. Your eight-year-old may not appreciate this, but no doubt, when interest peaks in that first boyfriend or girlfriend, they'll catch on pretty quick (and thank you later for being so cutting edge with your wisdom).

Also, for the record, we don't subscribe to the carrot theory. Sure, sometimes a little motivation is needed and a reward has been earned, but that's no substitute for instilling a personal sense of teamwork. A bribe or prize shouldn't be the stimulus for the actions your children take. It may serve an immediate need, but you're shortchanging them in the long run if they aren't taught the message in the bigger picture, which is to be part of the greater good. Build their character and deepen the goodness in their hearts. An unexpected surprise may deliver a well-deserved boost, but be sure to care for their hearts and heads first, not their wallets or their "want lists"! A pat on the back and positive words of affirmation can mean so much more. Teach them what truly counts most in all they do.

The Balancing Act

Moving right along! Your kids' rooms are in order and they have a sense of responsibility and commitment to the family team. The next area to tackle involves balance, and this one is a biggie, folks! The concept of balance spills into every area of your life and your children's lives. Almost everything is good in moderation—even chocolate and money! Unfortunately, though, even the good stuff taken to excess can be harmful. Too much of certain things can leave you feeling overwhelmed, anxious, and exhausted, and too little of others can render feelings of isolation, emptiness, and hopelessness. Either scenario breeds misery. The key is to address each area in the mix, make solid decisions as to what is or isn't necessary, and then act on the template of priority you establish. The less you leave to chance, the better. We firmly believe doing the work on the front side saves so much time and effort on the back.

So what does balance look like in the life of your youngsters? A healthy perspective and keeping it all in check is just as helpful in their lives as it is in yours, and they too need to declutter in order to manage their material possessions, activities, and social lives. It may be on a different scale than yours, but the concept is essentially the same.

Sensibility with Stuff

Do your kids have every stuffed animal or fast food kids' meal toy ever made? There isn't a friend's house we've visited where the parents aren't complaining about the abundance of toys as they give us the grand tour. It cracks us up when every parent says the exact same thing but continues to indulge in the unnecessary. Is this type of excess paramount to the happiness and development of your children? Of course not! A closet full of toys doesn't replace quality time spent with a parent and isn't an indicator of how much your children are loved. Remember, moderation! Kids should have a sensible selection (and don't ask us to define sensible, parents, we know you can do this!) of toys and games to choose from, preferably ones which promote creative thinking, life, and educational skills. They should also have some that are just plain fun, but anything above and beyond a limited, reasonable selection is total overkill.

Take time to periodically clean out the surplus. Perhaps make it a quarterly event where a donation is given to the local crisis shelter or other organization in need of children's items. A great piece of advice Sherry came across years ago is to tuck half of your toddler's toys away and then every month or so, rotate them back into the play cycle and store the other half away. To your toddler, it will seem as though they're getting a set of brand new toys every month and the limited selection will encourage them to enjoy what they have. Genius!

Years ago when my [Lindon's] son, Trent, was about four years old, I had a heck of a time getting him to part with the loads of stuffed animals that were breeding out of control in our home. Creativity was required because Trent was having no part of the suggestion to give some of them away. I was always bringing the animals to life for the kids and having impromptu puppet shows and just being goofy, so I decided to use this puppet play to make a point. I explained to Trent, while personifying the animals, they really weren't getting the love and attention they deserved if they were stuffed up in high nets and buried in huge garbage bags in the garage. Trent had a select few animals he played with which were extra special to him and, of course, he knew he was special to them as well. Aside from those, however, the rest were stored away, untouched. I explained there were young kids his age that didn't have any special animals, not even one. Wouldn't it be wonderful, I prompted, for some of his animals to be loved and taken really great care of *all* the time by kids like him, instead of being tucked away and ignored? He got it! Smart kid with a big heart! It took a little fancy footwork, but he was able to understand the value of sharing without a knock-down drag-out fight or terrible temper tantrum. I got to clean out unused toys and some deserving children got a special treat. These are the win-wins we should strive for.

Follow the same process with clothes. If your kids are like ours, they have a few favorite shirts or outfits which get worn to oblivion and the rest hang untouched in the closet, often with tags still on. Most kids outgrow clothes long before they have a chance to wear them out. Pass along the extra clothing to kids in need or gather them up for your next yard sale. Again, use this as a teaching moment. Bring your children with you when you make the clothing donation or enlist their help with the yard sale and allow them to share in the profits. Pump them up with all the fantastic reasons for keeping their room decluttered. A feeling of accomplishment and order, a greater appreciation for what they have, joy from giving to those less fortunate, a taste of the entrepreneurial spirit, and earning a few bucks can really encourage a youngster.

Dodging Destruction

Let's step out of the bedroom and into your kids' lives where balance is critical. How many activities are your children involved in? How many clubs, groups, sports teams, music, or band programs is your son or daughter actively participating in? Is their schedule overwhelming? Are they going, going, going with you in tow 24 / 7? If something changes, does the schedule get thrown so far off-kilter that recovery feels insurmountable? Is every minute orchestrated to such a degree and with such precision that the focus is how to manage it all rather than truly enjoying it? Do you feel like all you're doing is constantly hurrying and hollering for them to "get in the car, get in the car, get in the car..." only then to scream, "get out of the car, get out of the car, get out of the car!" We're almost chuckling as we write this but not so much because it's funny, but rather because we can hear ourselves, especially Sherry, saying these things and living this drama just a few short years ago. Is homework lagging in the priority list? Are there any available minutes for precious family time? Is there even time to be sick? Are there days and nights set aside just for downtime; simply to relax and "veg"?

We as parents, even with the best of intentions, are all too often guilty of not doing the best for our kids. We want our kids to be included. We want them to have fun. We want them to explore a multitude of activities because if they don't, how will they make educated decisions about what they like or dislike in the future? Surely they must experience it all, we rationalize. These appear to be sane arguments, but we believe them to be the greater of the evils.

Lindon likes to think of children as batteries. The more you extract from them, the quicker they burn out if they're not allowed to recharge. The objective shouldn't be for them to experience anything and everything available, but to truly enjoy each leg of their journey. If they actually have the opportunity to focus on what they're doing long enough to learn from it and form an educated opinion, they'll gain the insight and ability to make wise choices. Whether they were passionate or not about the activity isn't the point. It's the process which carries far more significance. Draining their battery won't do them a bit of good in any area, so provide the atmosphere and tools conducive for keeping them charged up through their experiences and watch them shine!

Where do you draw the line and how do you help each child balance his or her schedule? Use their individual strengths and weaknesses to guide your advice and decisions. It's a bummer, but there isn't a one-size-fits-all approach.

[*Sherry*] My son, Ryan, is the over-achieving type who was able to juggle a host of things at the same time. I was worried there was too much on his plate, so I addressed this with the school counselor who knew Ryan well. She suggested because of how Ry was driven, I would do him no service by insisting he limit his current six commitments to just three. She explained that with Ryan's personality and drive, he would work just as hard in three areas as he did in six, so if I was looking to accumulate more downtime, this wasn't the way to accomplish it. The counselor asked me if he was sleeping well. Was his demeanor and attitude positive? Was he eating properly and did he seem happy and healthy overall? The answer to all of the above was an emphatic yes. The counselor's advice was to allow Ryan to continue the track he was on and keep an eye on him. It was my job to make sure things continued on a positive path with the caveat that I was to incorporate some downtime and family time in the equation for balance. Another counselor suggested "planned spontaneity" in Ry's schedule, an oxymoron if I ever heard one, but I understood the advice. Ryan could handle the load, and as long as there wasn't a toll being taken on him or the family, all systems were go.

As the last paragraph was being written, Ryan happened to walk in the room. I asked him if he enjoyed the chaos of his youth. He truly was a busy kid! He was involved in sports, band, student government, church, and Boy Scouts. Did he enjoy the crazy, constant forward motion as much as he said he did way back when? His answer was unequivocally yes! If you asked me now, I would say in hindsight we had too much going on and we would have benefited from a little more wiggle room in our lives. But at least he has no regrets, and I don't feel guilty as a mom. If the situation warranted it, or had the counselor's advice been different, I wouldn't have hesitated to make the tough and unpopular calls. This is why we get paid the big bucks—because our children don't always know what's best for them!

Revealing the Root

What if your children are over-involved but don't want to be, or are participating in activities they would rather not be part of? If this is the case, what's propelling them down this path? Our kids, just like us, can be guilty of trying to keep up with their friends or succumbing to peer pressure. Perhaps a desire to please you is driving your kids to ramp up their involvement? Do you yearn for them to keep up with other families or to do what the popular kids are doing? Does this guilt them into making the wrong decisions? Help your children to declutter this area of their lives if need be. This may be a bit difficult for you, however, if you're responsible for causing any of the clutter, so let's dissect this a bit further.

Take an honest inventory of the reasons surrounding your children's involvements, and ask yourself if you're herding them into areas you either fell short or excelled in. Is this causing you to overlook what's in their best interests or to ignore their desires? Are you trying to live your missed opportunities through them, or do you want your children to follow in your footsteps? If your children do gravitate towards your childhood passion, more power to you, but don't make the mistake of allowing your wants to supersede theirs. We'd all like our kids to have some of our interests or participate in activities we did in our youth. It's a heartwarming feeling to dust off your old Bari Sax and watch your kid perform with it on stage at the fall band concert. We get it! Just make sure your youngster is as excited about it as you are!

Do you encourage a particular sport because there's a "darn good scholarship opportunity if you keep it up?" This is not a legitimate reason for your children to spend years doing something they don't enjoy. Perhaps you desire your teenager to be well-rounded and skilled in a variety of things. While this may be a good idea in theory, if your teen isn't enjoying the experiences, it won't be so positive in actuality.

[*Sherry*] I endured a particularly painful experience which will illustrate part of the point we're trying to drive home. Ryan decided, after a successful grade and high school baseball career, to forego playing varsity ball his senior year in high school. Really? Are you kidding me? This could have been a crowning moment for him (and me?). As a solid lefty pitcher and player, senior ball might have well been the catalyst for playing college ball. Besides, I had my group of baseball parents to hang with and looked forward to each and every game. Aside from being proud of Ry and enjoying watching him play, it was my social time and there was no way I wanted to be left out of all the senior year fun. I have to admit there were many mornings when I drove by the baseball team practicing and welled up with tears because I missed it all so much. To those of you who aren't wired this way, this is an absurd notion, but for those like-minded sports parents, I bet you can feel the pit in my stomach and the lump in my throat. It was awful! Thanks be to God I had the sense and strength to keep my mouth shut. Ryan knew I would've preferred that he played baseball, but I didn't guilt, badger, or coerce him into it. He ended up making the varsity men's volleyball team and had an absolute ball (pun intended). If I'm being honest, I did too. It made his last year in high school memorable and unique. Do you enjoy sitting in the stands more than your children like being on the field? If so, release your selfish interest and guide your children through their decluttering process so they can find what makes them happy.

If you're not guilty of any of these behaviors, can you recognize the parents who are? We sure can! They're the ones who seem far more excited about the game than their kids do and are overbearing, overzealous, and way too serious about it all. We've known them and witnessed their poor conduct and attitude. It usually isn't pretty. They're the parents who get noticed for all the wrong reasons and are whispered about when their backs are turned. "Did you see how Frank just yelled at his daughter?" or "I feel so bad for little Tyler having to go home with his mom. She's a bossy nightmare!" The kids appear stressed out, unhappy, and uninterested in being there. Their parents are often too proud or self-absorbed to admit it or realize it, but they embarrass their kids. It's an unnecessary and preventable agony for your sons or daughters, and it carries with it detrimental, long-term ramifications.

Disabling vs. Enabling

Our plan for this chapter was to encourage parents to get their kids to declutter from the get-go. As we alluded to earlier, it really has as much to do with you as it does them and, in part, involves decluttering yourself from their lives as needed. The previous section was one example, but we have a few more.

We've seen, in the course of dealing with our kids' friends and families, parents who do TOO much—sometimes way, way, way too much! The instigator is often, but not always, the children being overwhelmed and overloaded. The "assistance" the parents lend might be born from true concern and love, but that doesn't make it right. We've known parents who make phone calls their kids should be making, type reports their kids should be typing, and solve problems their kids should be solving. This prevents their children from achieving their potential and robs them of the tools they'll need to be successful. We have both heard about little Bobby who was just too exhausted from band practice and a basketball game in the same night to do his homework, so his mom completed the research for him. It was just the research for crying out loud; it's not like she wrote the whole paper by herself. Give us a break! There are no situations and no excuses legitimate enough to warrant this type of action. Lending assistance when your children have put their best foot forward is an act of love, but preventing challenges and fixing everything that's broken is destructive.

The term "helicopter parent" refers to parents who hover over, obsess, interfere with, and micro-manage every aspect of their kids' lives. This must be maddening for little, let's call her Ellie. At the very least, if Ellie takes advantage of all the helicopter parent has to offer, she's being set up, unknowingly, for a lifetime of dependence, frustration, and disappointment. Pity Ellie's future husband who will have a high-maintenance, low-skilled wife on his hands. Or her kids who will be trained early on that they have an obligation to serve and take care of their mother. Remember when we said kids shouldn't be born with a job waiting for them? This is a prime case in point.

Have you ever heard the term "fire-putter-outer"? Not grammatically correct per se, but an authentic noun referring to parents who metaphorically run ahead and strategically lay the groundwork to "put out any fires," a.k.a. fix any problems, before the child happens upon the situation. When the child actually arrives, everything's under control and the chance of Billy being disappointed, hurt, or having to work too hard has been neutralized. Have you known parents who "love too much"? Sometimes our kids need to fail. As much as it pains us to watch them go through it, they need to experience challenge, hurt, and regret. If they don't, how can we teach them to brush their knees off and get up again?

How about the child who is excited about joining a team or group, has mom and dad purchase all the equipment and goodies, and then decides after two practices it's too much work or they don't like it? Unless there is a health or otherwise critical reason your child should quit, we firmly believe they must be taught the value of commitment by being required to complete the season or class. Help your kids to make informed decisions to eliminate the chance of "buyer's remorse," but if it occurs, insist they finish what they start. You will be doing them a great service and instilling lifelong values.

Parents, we unapologetically make our case but it's not to be harsh or insensitive. Quite the opposite. We want you motivated to get this right before it's too late, before your children are grown and gone, before you are riddled with regret. We don't want you, unknowingly, to add to your children's clutter in the way only a parent can. It's better to go out on a limb now and speak truth in the best way we can, than to miss the chance to share what we believe is vital for everyone involved.

So, as hard as it may be for you, mom and dad, don't extract from your children's' lives the essential tools they'll need for a successful future. Of course you don't want them to go through difficult and painful times, but it's a process they must endure which will develop their abilities and bolster their confidence. Decluttering will help your children clear out the excess and unnecessary, however, it's just as important to make sure you aren't taking away what they *do* need. This is the balance we're talking about. Just like knowing what to keep and what to let go, your children also need to learn when to say yes and when to say no. We, as parents, have to distinguish between when to help and when to step back. This is no small task!

We recently did a study with our small group on the Fruit of the Spirit and learned a great truth regarding God's position on self-control. Think about how God felt knowing what his only Son was about to endure. Can you even imagine the self-control he had to exert in not rescuing Jesus from the horrific pain and suffering he endured? God had the power to stop the crucifixion, to get Jesus off the cross immediately or, better yet, to keep him from being crucified. Put yourself in God's position. Can you relate to having the power to rescue your child but being disciplined enough to hold back for the greater good? We would do well to follow God's lead.

Social Snares

The necessity of balance in your kids' social lives is just as critical. How much time do your children spend on the phone talking or texting, on the computer, in front of the TV, or playing video games? Is it excessive and all consuming? Do they spend a crazy amount of time with the same person or have a steady stream of back-to-back sleepovers? Take a look at the different areas in which your children spend their time and evaluate if you think it meets healthy, reasonable standards. Don't leave it up to your twelve-year-old to tell you, "Well, Mom, I've been on the computer way too much lately, and I think I need to make an effort to refrain from the internet. I find it distracting to my studies and disruptive to my family life." If you're expecting to hear this, you may be in for a rude awakening! While there are exceptions, and some kids have self-discipline and maturity far beyond their years, this isn't the norm. For the majority, specific boundaries need to be established. These activities, in managed moderation, can play a positive role in helping your children relax, recharge, and have fun, but the key is moderation. Take a hands-on posture and spearhead the effort to teach your children to establish and maintain a healthy balance.

The Greatest Parent of All

You may be wondering where the wisdom in our advice comes from. We do have four kids between us and a whole lot of parenting under our belts, but the truth of the matter is we have gleaned much of what we know from the best teacher of all, our Heavenly Father. Think about it. Who better to learn from than the one responsible for setting the ultimate parenting standard and example? God treats us just as he wants us to treat our kids, so if we just follow his lead, we'll be in good shape! He clearly wants us to imitate him in every way. He's worthy of being emulated and we would do well to follow this directive. What does God say that would support the advice we've shared with you throughout this chapter?

We are given comprehensive and sound examples from God and are to give comprehensive and sound examples to our children: "Be imitators of God, therefore, as dearly loved children and live a life of love, just as Christ loved us and gave himself up for us as a fragrant offering and sacrifice to God" (Eph. 5:1-2).

We are cared for by God and are to care for our children: "Cast all your anxiety on him because he cares for you" (1 Pet. 5:7). God doesn't weigh us down with his problems. It's a silly notion to even think about it in those terms, isn't it? He asks us to bring our anxiety to him, not the other way around. In the same spirit, we aren't to share or pass along our stress to our kids. Instead, we're to help them with their stress and provide a safe environment and understanding ear. We want them to feel comfortable bringing their burdens to us as their parents, just as God did for us as his children. Not only will this help us build a strong relationship with our children, but down the road when they're teenagers and honest communication comes at a premium, we'll stand a far better chance of being included rather than shut out.

We are protected by God and are to protect our children. Have you ever read Psalm 91? If you haven't, please do. Even if you have, take a fresh look and refresh the verses in your mind. The theme of the entire passage is how God is our shelter, our refuge. While the author isn't referring to shelter in the physical sense, this concept certainly applies to that aspect as well. God provides a place for us where we feel safe from our fears. Our kids should also be privy to the reassurance of protection. This should come not only in the form of emotional protection but from our home, a structural shield from the perils of life, a place where the ills stay outside the doorway and aren't allowed to enter in.

We are taught by God and are to teach our children. "Take my yoke upon you and learn from me…" (Mt. 11:29). "This is what the Lord says—your Redeemer, the Holy One of Israel: 'I am the Lord your God, who teaches you what is best for you, who directs you in the way you should go'" (Isa. 48:17). God equips us by making sure all the lessons he wants us to learn are available to us for the asking, and even sometimes, when we don't ask. We are to do the same for our kids. They may not be open to each lesson, nor will they always be in the frame of mind to listen when we're in the mindset to teach, but we aren't to allow that to deter us. We have invaluable experiences and wisdom to share, and just as God offers this to us without hesitation, fear or obligation, we must extend the same to our children.

We are disciplined by God and are to discipline our children. "…
My son, do not make light of the Lord's discipline, and do not lose heart
when he rebukes you, because the Lord disciplines those he loves, and
he punishes everyone he accepts as a son" (Heb. 12:5-6). No discipline
is pleasant when it's being handed out, and we don't know many people
who enjoy being corrected or punished, but God's discipline is a sign of
his deep love for us. As God's actions have shown, he believes it's best to
teach, correct, and sometimes even punish. We must show the same love
and effort to our kids. They may not initially see it as such, nor will they
enjoy it, but encourage them to see the lesson in the discipline and not to
focus on the discipline itself.

God gives us verse after verse to show what we need, as well as setting the pace on how we are to behave. To love, show compassion, nurture, encourage, be patient, be kind, set boundaries, lead by example,
be unselfish, etc.—we could go on and on. The answer to any question
we have and the standard for any behavior required is all in the Bible.
Every thought and question is addressed. We can't stump God. Ever!
Check it out and you'll be amazed the plethora of phenomenal advice
and wisdom which is offered. God was and clearly is the greatest parent
of all and the "Master Declutterer"! He had it all figured out and under
control long before the phrase was coined and the concept brought to
you through Declutter Now! Follow his lead and teach your children to
follow him as well.

Charge to Parents

Parents are commanded to bring their children up in the way of
the Lord. Christian parents want their children to know Christ. They
long for their children's salvation. They desire their children to rely on a

God who is always loving, always truthful, always dependable, and always just. Desire alone, as you might imagine, is not enough. Parents must do the work to make it happen. Take your kids to church, enroll them in Sunday School classes, talk to them about God, incorporate prayer into your lives on a daily basis, and surround them with God's love in all you do. Teaching your children to declutter and stay that way is beneficial in and of itself, but the ultimate objective is for the same for them as it is for you—to be able to enjoy the freedom to serve God. At the end of the day, that's what it's all about.

No discussion concerning raising children would be complete without the following:

"Train a child in the way he should go, and when he is old he will not turn from it" (Prov. 22:6). God clearly spells out the importance of training your children well. He knows it will affect their entire lives, and he wants you to get it right, for them and for yourself. There's no more important, or all-encompassing gift you can give your children.

We began this chapter by suggesting that as your children grow responsibility should gradually shift from your shoulders to theirs. Equally, if not more imperative, is for your children to shift their dependence on you to a dependence on God. Let that sink in for a moment; the significance of this cannot be overstated. They must understand that while being responsible is a necessary part of their earthly maturity and growth, depending on Christ with all their heart, mind, body, and soul is essential for their spiritual maturity and growth.

Enable your kids to declutter so they can successfully navigate the challenges of life. Teach them from the beginning so they don't have the big work later. We, as parents, have a crucial place in our kids' lives, but do them a favor and know your place! Establish and abide by healthy boundaries personally, so you remain in a position to do your job well. Model by example and set a positive pattern to emulate. As your children grow, mature, and become more responsible, your role must shift. As they progress forward, you need to step back! At some point, you'll have to overcome the most difficult task of all and release them to fly, but if you've been successful, they'll never be alone. They will know the Lord their God is with them and will never abandon nor fail them. Parents, it's perfectly reasonable and acceptable to stick around and support, reinforce, and oversee as they make their way, but we are certain you'd rather do this with pride in your heart for what they're accomplishing, as opposed to heart-wrenching regret and guilt for where you failed them. Yes, there will be bumps in the road for your kids, but stumbling, brushing their knees off, relying on God, re-charting their course, and giving it another go is a far cry from failing because they're incapable and completely ill-prepared.

We are all, in some way, shape or form, always "under construction." We are all a work in progress. Declutter your parental life and then assist your kids in decluttering the unnecessary, excess, and overwhelming from their own lives. Provide for them all they're entitled to, including a home life and relationship with you where love, respect, and drama-free living are valued and promoted. Be parents who make the time and effort to understand your children's needs and preferences. Set boundaries, teach balance, and require responsibility. Inspire them to live clutter-free and with intentionality and purpose. Be wise and diligent in handing down the lessons and tools your children will need. Introduce them to their Lord and Savior, Jesus Christ. Encourage and nurture their relationship with him and their heart for service. And lead by example! Set them up for their greatest chance of success. Have the peace of knowing that when you're gone, you've given them the best present of all: the opportunity for a bright, prosperous, and healthy future and the freedom to serve a God who will be with them forever and ever. AMEN.

Chapter 7

Mind Over What Doesn't Matter

"[Jesus] answered, 'Love the Lord your God with
all your heart and with all your soul and with all
your strength and with all your mind...'"

(Luke 10:27).

THERE'S NO BETTER CHAPTER IN this book that exemplifies why the freedom attained in decluttering is so important. How can you love God with all your mind, if your mind is a cluttered, stressed-out, and burdened mess? The short answer, of course, is you can't. There is much you can do to repair this, but your mental state—an abstract, intangible part of your being—often gets relegated to the backburner, remaining unchallenged and unfixed. The effects of this state, whether positive or negative, can produce concrete results, but since you can't touch or feel what propels the energy, it's both difficult to detect and easy to ignore a problem, especially if you aren't looking. We'll bring to light some common hurdles that will prompt you to evaluate your current state of mind. Chances are you're dealing with a few of them right now, but even if you're not, prepare to heighten your awareness so potential problems can be addressed before they become irreparable or destructive patterns.

Who among us doesn't suffer from stress, anxiety, worry, mental overload, discontentment, or depression from time to time? We say no one. There is a substantial difference, though, between having a bad moment or even a bad day and drowning in a cycle of repetitive, draining mental meltdowns. While they both deserve our attention, it's the latter that we're most concerned with. The world views stress as a normal part of everyday life, but then in the same breath offers dozens of pills to aid you in overcoming its incapacitating effects. "Normal" doesn't sound so appealing!

"Do not conform any longer to the pattern of this world, but be transformed by the renewing of your mind…" (Rom. 12:2). In this verse, Paul is referring to the renewing of our minds for Jesus Christ. He wants us to transform from the ways of the world and live for him. Consider the word "renew," which means to reestablish, restore to freshness, and to make like new. How energizing would it be to declutter all the garbage we mentally deal with, wipe the slate clean, start fresh, and remain in that brilliance? Say that last sentence out loud. Just speaking it feels like a step in the right direction, doesn't it? Let's embark on the next leg of this decluttering journey.

Stressology

In Chapter 5 Temple Care and Maintenance, we highlighted the physical ramifications of stress (those scary lists of diseases and debilitating conditions), but let's delve into how stress can demonize your mind and your life. Stress occurs when forces, whether internal or external, affect an individual. We often think of stress as negative, but there are cases when stress can be motivating and increase productivity. For instance, running a race or being involved in an election can produce good stress, which in reasonable doses, is beneficial.

Harmful stress is the bigger concern and the type of stress that breeds long-term anxiety, depression, and worry. Left untreated, it can become completely debilitating and life-altering. Both of us have felt the ramifications of stress, and we've each had to work through a variety of difficult circumstances to come out on top. God doesn't want us carrying our burdens on our own shoulders, and implores us to give them to him. That almost sounds too good to be true, doesn't it? He willingly bears the weight of our struggles. Who would offer to do this? Our faithful, loving, and strong God does! He begs us to bring our afflictions, our load, to his feet and allow him to work in our lives and carry the weight on our behalf. Psalm 68:19 assures us that the Lord "daily bears our burdens." If he's going to do this anyway, there is no point in carrying our own burdens as well, right?

Visualize this scenario. You're walking next to Jesus fighting with him over your burdens. "I've got it, I've got it," you say. "No, let me take it," Jesus responds. You counter, "I said it's mine; I got it covered. I want to keep my problems for myself." "No precious child, I'm here for you. Please give me your problems and allow me to carry them for you."

Get the picture? We can think of a few things that might cause us to tussle with God, but fighting over our problems isn't one of them. Definitely not in the top ten! In this case, there's no point being stubborn or greedy. Give it all up to him! Unfortunately, as logical as it may sound, handing your stress over to God often proves to be no small task. Denial, ignorance, stubbornness, control issues, etc., are just some of the roadblocks that can trip you up and thwart your reliance on him.

[*Sherry*] I was seriously depressed for a day and a half. Before you roll your eyes, start laughing, and make fun, hear me out. I'd never felt depression, nor could I relate to it, so this was an eye-opening, profound learning experience. Brief as it was, it made a lifelong impression.

A few years back I was working through an extremely difficult situation. I was challenged by God to change the way I regarded my ex-husband. I was often quite critical of him and never viewed him through Christ-filled eyes of love, mercy, or grace. I'm not proud of this, but it's the ugly truth. I could rationalize and say his actions earned my harsh judgment and I was justified, but even if true, his behavior shouldn't have dictated how I, as a Christian, behaved. Ephesians 4:32 tells us to be kind and compassionate to one another; forgiving each other, just as in Christ God forgave you. This verse doesn't tell us to be kind if the recipient deserves it or has earned our respect. Nope, God just directs us in how we are called to act with no qualifiers attached.

Some background will be helpful. When the marriage ended years prior, the relationship did not. Back and forth we'd go in an unhealthy and hurtful cycle. After our last "break up," my sister Deborah suggested one last ditch effort to repair the relationship. (We both ignored the fact that I had been divorced forever at this point!) Her argument was that I'd spent over a dozen years getting it wrong and, if I was throwing in the towel for good anyway, what harm could it do to try a completely different approach? She proposed that I wipe the slate clean, be as nonjudgmental as my human self would allow, let my guard down, and just enjoy being with him. No stress or obligation, and no holding on to old hurts or preconceived notions. While I wasn't optimistic about this new approach (and for me, this surely would be new!), it was intriguing. Not a very sincere motive, but since my ex readily agreed, I decided to give it a try.

While I was half-hearted in my initial response, I committed to putting forth a 110% effort and can honestly say that's precisely what I did. I prayed that God would remove the scales from my eyes and allow me to view my ex-husband through Christ's eyes. I prayed to be delivered from my critical and judgmental nature, and I petitioned God for a work of healing and restoration. I prayed for us to have fun, to be filled with peace, and to experience a fresh start. Inside of a month I had it, legitimately had it all. It was the craziest situation but I knew it was straight from God because only he could have worked such a miracle. I still had reservations, but things were going exceptionally well. I was letting loose, enjoying myself, and basking in his attention and the renewed hope. He seemed to be doing exactly the same.

Shortly after that first month, my ex-husband changed radically. He became increasingly vocal about his unresolved bitterness toward me. He grew more distant and guarded, less attentive and affectionate. His fuse was shorter, in fact shorter than anything I'd experienced from him even when our marriage was failing. Confusion doesn't adequately begin to describe how I felt. Our relationship had appeared to be going incredibly well, and the change in direction was abrupt and frightening. I was in a position completely foreign to me; I was vulnerable. I had shared with him what God had been teaching me since we started "dating" again. I apologized for things I'd never owned before and made promises I'd never been willing to commit to. I showed him an unprecedented grace and forgiveness. Now this? I felt sucker-punched, helpless, and painfully exposed.

Still, I didn't sway. This time I wasn't quitting. I took the verbal lashings and emotional abuse. Was this my penance for my previous behavior? When things got worse, I hung on even tighter. One night, in particular, was horrific. I was berated for almost two hours, reprimanded for every offense I'd ever committed against him, some of which I didn't even remember. The messages my head was sending me became increasingly convoluted and I prayed for God to tell me what to do. I hadn't hurt this much before, even while going through the divorce. I had finally let my guard down enough to allow God's vision and love to positively impact how I saw another, and it was proving to be one of the most dreadful experiences of my life. And I had willingly signed up for this? Ugh!

I found out my ex had lied about a few things; his heart grew cold and he seemed increasingly unreachable. The decision I should've made seemed like a no-brainer, but that's precisely the problem with depression—you can't see clearly. I was sinking. I went to work but couldn't concentrate, and each day after work became a cry fest. I couldn't take it anymore. One day I left work early and just crumpled on my couch. My body felt like it weighed 1000 pounds and my heart felt bruised, literally. My shoulders slumped and I couldn't even move my arms. They felt like lead weights hanging off my body. I wanted to stay holed up in my four walls forever and left alone to my misery. I wanted the world to go away. This behavior was so out of character for me and I was embarrassed for anyone to know how weak and helpless I'd become. I was numb with grief and overcome with pain. I called in to work the next day. The thought of mustering the strength to shower and get dressed was more than I could bear. The bathroom was at the end of a long, gloomy hallway that would narrow as I walked. I didn't have the energy to consider starting the journey. I was exhausted, and I know I scared Ryan. I was the president of the stoic "Never Say Die" club. My condition had him worried; I was worried too.

My ex-husband didn't care. It was almost as if he fed off my pain. Oddly enough, I realized I wasn't crying over him or even the relationship. Huh? I know! That was a surprise to me too! You see, as much as he hurt my feelings and bruised my pride, that wasn't the worst part. It was more distressing to have finally learned lessons I so desperately needed, administered directly from the hand of God, and now that I was a star student (or so I thought!), it seemed God was teasing me and not allowing me the chance to utilize them. It was maddening to finally feel like I was getting it and then have the door of opportunity with which to utilize my new skills shut so abruptly. I wanted to show God what I could do, darn it, and I'd convinced myself this was my chance! Ahhhh, clearly still more lessons to learn!

Stacy, my best friend whom I had drug along on every step of this wild ride, pleaded that I speak to my pastor. After some coaxing, I agreed. I'd been debating whether I should be obedient and endure the punishment to receive some glorious payoff for my restitution efforts, or if I was being shown it was time to move on from the guilt and pain I'd come to wear as a badge of pity. If only I had a crystal ball. Can you relate? It was unchartered water for this headstrong, independent woman to be riddled with so much confusion. But God had a plan, and he delivered me.

While I was getting ready for the appointment with my pastor, the Holy Spirit clearly and simply said, "Sherry, God doesn't speak in riddles." Those six words set me free and changed my life forever. The Holy Spirit

196 | *Declutter Now!*

is our crystal ball, and we must open our ears and heart to hear him. I knew in that instant that God wasn't trying to cloud my thoughts with confusing messages, tempt me with open doors that were a gateway to harm, or inflict pain as a payback. He didn't want me mistreated, abused, and miserable. God wouldn't have made it this hard to be happy. He doesn't speak in riddles, and he wanted me to move on. It was time. He taught me what I needed and then slammed that door shut in a mighty way. God is so faithful.

When I met with the pastor, he reaffirmed what I'd been told by the Holy Spirit that morning, even before I shared with him the word I had received. He said that God used someone I loved very much to get to my heart and expose my shortcomings, but this was to be for good, not for suffering. He suggested I must put down the bag of guilt I'd slung over my shoulder for years and break free from the past. God had broken me down, and it was time to rebuild. His counsel made so much sense and left me filled with peace and hope. I knew God had something wondrous in mind for me.

After I left the pastor's office, I was able to thank God for loving me enough to spend so much time on me. That was a first. Never before had I thanked him for a lesson that was jam-packed with so much agony. Through my suffering, God shared with me a bigger picture. I never called my ex again, nor looked back. Each morning when I woke and chose to walk in God's light, I was a step closer to where he wanted me to be. It was an incredible experience that instilled a faith that I will appreciate forever. Just four months later when Lindon prayed before dinner on our first date, I knew he was the man God intended for me. He was to be blessed with all I'd learned and all I had to give. I knew this with more certainty than anything I'd ever known before and I've thanked God every day since for his wisdom, persistence, and overwhelming love.

The day and a half spent on the couch was terrifying. I caught a mere glimpse of life-altering depression. Truth be told, I was probably depressed for many weeks leading up to that, but those few moments etched a lifetime of learning into my heart. My journey had delivered generous doses of stress, anxiety, worry, agony, and pain; I don't think there was a negative emotion I didn't experience. Those feelings were so completely crushing and so totally overpowering, they destroyed any prospect for normalcy outside of my narrow focus. I was utterly self-consumed, rendering me of no use to anyone, including God. I loved God with my whole heart, but the emotional stress I was under robbed me of any opportunity to put my love into action for his kingdom. Doesn't that defeat the entire purpose of why we are here to begin with? "But be sure to fear the LORD and serve him faithfully with all your heart; consider what great things he has done for you" (1 Sam. 12:24). We are asked to have our whole heart and mind available for his service, and decluttering them is a step closer to that end.

Forgive and Forget

There are other emotions that can clutter your mind and hinder you as well. Anger and jealousy are tremendous joy-stealers. Are you one to hold grudges or bathe in resentment? These feelings and behaviors permeate your being with bitterness and hatefulness that swallow up any chance you might have for a healthy, happy existence. We often mistake holding on to hurt as a shield of vindication, but this is severely misguided. Instead of being protected behind our armor, we end up being bound to the pain by perpetuating the hurt in our lives. It's a double-edged sword. Not only do we take our pain out on our offender, but we are miserable ourselves. How do we declutter this deep-rooted, destructive emotion? It's a challenging task to be sure, but not an impossible one. Jesus has given us an abundance of clear instructions and examples that we'll lean on to light our way.

Forgiveness of others is a huge part of the equation and one of the most difficult sentiments to master. We, in all our humanness, have hearts that love and feel deeply, and when we are hurt, these wounds run just as deep. Our pastor spoke on forgiving recently and shared a profoundly impactful point. When we forgive someone as God calls us to do, we aren't implying that it was okay that we were hurt. We aren't agreeing that the infraction against us was called for or deserved. We are simply trying to love others as God loves us. If you think about it, that's exactly how God operates. When we sin against him, he doesn't respond with, "Eh, it's no problem. No big deal." He never condones our wrongdoing but forgives us through his mercy and grace. In our obedience to God, we would do well to emulate his example.

The dictionary definition of "forgive" is to excuse for a fault or an offense, to renounce anger or resentment against, to grant relief from payment of, to pardon. Not surprisingly, the definition falls short of the Bible's instruction and fail to address WHY we should forgive. Thank goodness for God's Word that guides and directs us. He tells us to forgive simply because Christ forgave us and, when we do, we will receive blessings. "Bear with each other and forgive whatever grievances you may have against one another. Forgive as the Lord forgave you" (Col. 3:13).

Did you have a parent whose standard response was, "because I said so"? We think everyone has heard that once or twice! God goes much further than that. He leads by example and asks us to follow in his footsteps. It's a lot easier to honor someone's wishes with respect when the one instructing us has already done the work we are being asked to perform. In addition, God tells us that if we do as he asks, there will be a reward. "Do not repay evil with evil or insult with insult, but with blessing, because to this you were called so that you may inherit a blessing" (1 Pet. 3:9). Hallelujah! This directive doesn't suggest that we have to be thrilled about what we are feeling pain over. It doesn't demand that we agree with what was done. It simply coaches us to walk in the light of Jesus, treat others as he treats us, and if we do this, God will bless us. We can forgive, release someone of their debt to us, and without excuse or expectation simply feel pride in our actions as they serve a greater good.

Members in our small group discussed this, and the consensus was that prayer is the most powerful tool we have when seeking to extend forgiveness. It can soften our heart and pave the way for healing. Even if you agree, how in the world can you pray for someone who has undeniably and unconscionably wronged and profoundly wounded you? I [Sherry] have a particularly tough time with this. Last year, one of the members gave some advice that has stuck with me ever since. Lori said that God knows our hearts, and if we're trying to pray for someone who is so unlovable to us that the thought is nauseating, simply pray their name. That's it. Just the name. If you can't bring yourself to speak it, just think it! God will know exactly what to do with your offering. In time, perhaps, you can increase the prayer bit by bit, but at least you're heading in the right direction. God will get you the rest of the way. What great advice!

Lindon has the gift of "forgetting," which has set him free time and time again from being bound by negative clutter. It may help to remember that God does not just forgive us, but he actually "forgets" our sins and transgressions. It's not that he isn't smart enough to remember all of them. Hardly! It's merely that when he forgives us, he erases our wrongdoing and gives us a clean slate. He frees us. Isaiah 43:25 tells us, "I, even I, am he who blots out your transgressions, for my own sake, and remembers your sins no more." Jeremiah 31:34 says, "...For I will forgive their wickedness and will remember their sins no more." And Hebrews 10:17 reaffirms this, "...Their sins and lawless acts I will remember no more."

God isn't keeping score while waiting for the worst and expecting us to fail again, but that's exactly what we often do to our offenders. God gives us all the freedom we need to start fresh every day, even knowing that we'll mess up time and time again. How freeing would it be to declutter your feelings of anger and bitterness, thereby releasing not only your own heart and mind, but also that of your offender's? Talk about paying a gift forward! God would love nothing more, so do it for yourself and for God's sake too.

Make No Mistake?

Ahhhh...but the problem is that we do make mistakes—over and over again. It's part of our human nature that we continually wrestle with. We lament over the mess ups, bad choices, and instances where we beg God for a do-over. We regret actions that have brought us shame, guilt, and humiliation. Sometimes we attempt to avoid these feelings by unjustly pointing the finger at another, but that only serves to compound and perpetuate our wrongdoing. To be solely responsible, or at least feel that we are, for a major screw-up can be ego shattering, heartbreaking, and just plain devastating.

Are you besieged by remnants of this type of fallout not dealt with? Perhaps it has been buried deeper and deeper over the years but never resolved. ***There isn't enough dirt around to keep a good hurt down.*** Eventually, at some time or some place, whatever feelings you're trying to suppress will come roaring to the surface. Just as devastating is the reality that while these feelings appear to be buried, they are still constantly affecting your life, decisions, relationships, career, and joy every day. This seemingly sleeping giant is no sleeper at all and, when fully awake, will release a life-shattering and potentially destroying roar.

Have you ever felt that you are your own worst enemy? Your harshest critic? We are both guilty of this behavior. Why are we so hard on ourselves? We want to be successful, help others, advance at work, be a super mom or dad, etc., but often in this endeavor, we lose sight of the good we're doing along the way and focus on our blunders.

If you are called to forgive and forget others, don't you suspect that God also intended that to apply to you as well? Absolutely he did! You are to forgive because you have been forgiven. We aren't advising that it's acceptable to mess up, pretend you're sorry, half-heartedly ask for forgiveness, and then do it over and over again. That would be completely missing the mark. What we're encouraging is to give yourself the grace to learn from the error of your ways and move on. Unfortunately, scars from mistakes are often worn loud and proud, sometimes out of spite or arrogance, but more often as a result of feeling embarrassed, ashamed, and so terribly sorry. If you don't want to be stuck in perpetual limbo, you must allow yourself to be excused from your transgressions. Learn from your experience and do your best not to make the same mistake again. But the first step is to forgive yourself.

"Never be ashamed of the scars that life has left you
with. A scar means the hurt is over, the wound is closed,
you endured the pain, and God has healed you"

(author unknown).

Think about it from another angle. To forgive not only means to pardon for a fault or offense, but it also means to give up the desire to punish and to stop feeling angry or resentful toward someone (yourself?) for a flaw or mistake. Let's face it. Sometimes beating yourself up just feels so good. You deserve to be miserable, darn it! You earned your suffering and suffer you will, right? Wrong! That would be your next mistake and prideful to the core. Don't complicate one problem with another and assume you know better than God how to handle regret.

"If we confess our sins, he is faithful and just and will forgive us our sins and purify us from all unrighteousness" (1 John 1:9). We could list dozens of verses on forgiving; the Bible is far from silent on the issue. God is adamant about forgiving the offender, even when the one guilty of the offense is you. Confess your sins to God, let him do a work of healing in your life, and free yourself from the guilt and shame of sin.

A Mind Is a Terrible Thing to Clutter

Our mind is vital to our being and plays such a chief role in all we are, yet we continually bog it down with hoards of unnecessary and unproductive junk. How many shoppers are out there? I [*Sherry*] am not what you might consider a fanatical shopper, but when I go, I go big. I want just the right item at a reasonable cost and, for clothing, it must fit perfectly. In the interest of accomplishing this, I generally drive myself crazy. I'll spend half the day in a single store trying to put together one outfit I like. It's sheer madness. This will include, but isn't limited to, hours in the dressing room, trying and retrying on clothing, and comparing different brands and prices. If I'm fortunate enough to find something I like, I then set about the task of selecting what color looks best, while also considering how much I have of each color already so I don't disrupt the wardrobe balance I've worked hard to establish. When success occurs, it's then time to start on the accessories. *Oy vey!* The upside to my lunacy is I leave little room for buyer's remorse. However, the process is over the top and utterly mentally and physically draining. Why do I allow this? WHY?

What are some decisions you've allowed to consume far more energy and brain cells that they are worthy of? Granted, we all have important decisions to make from time to time, but even those should be surrounded by healthy boundaries. There's a time to evaluate and consider, and then a time to pull the trigger and make a decision. A lawyer once told Sherry that being on the middle of the fence is the worst place to be. You have no answer and no life while you're hanging in limbo. If you make a choice and it's the right one, more power to you for jumping down onto the correct side. However, if you jump down on the wrong side, you'll at least then know it was wrong and have the opportunity to get to the right side. Either way, the eternal debate ends.

Mental overload is incapacitating. While decluttering your mind isn't a physical action, it'll have concrete, positive results. Here's a simple illustration. Let's say you have the day off work and you plan to utilize this time to get caught up. You have errands to run, phone calls to make, bills to pay, and cleaning to be done. You wake up with anxiety over the enormity of your tasks at hand; there is much to do and limited time to accomplish it. We've all been there.

If you start out like a chicken with its head cut off, you're never going to make good use of your time, and you'll likely not enjoy much of your day. Chances are you'll miss a stop when running your errands and have to backtrack or forget some errands altogether. You may start power cleaning before an appointment and then realize you have to rush to make it on time, finally showing up late, disheveled, and sweaty. When you're bogged down and not thinking clearly, you make poor choices, your efforts can feel backwards or half done and, at the end of the day, you likely feel discouraged and unsuccessful. Decluttering your mind won't give you less to do, but it'll give you the edge up on getting it accomplished. Wouldn't you rather feel a sense of control in managing tasks and pride in a day well done, than to feel riddled with angst and disappointment?

We are big list makers. Sometimes we joke that we have lists for our lists, but it's a great tool for organizing and increasing effectiveness. Have you ever been so consumed with all there is to be done that the to-do list swirls around non-stop in your head? Write it down! If you make a list, you can purge the information from your brain but it won't be lost. You can organize better and feel a sense of triumph each time you check something off the list. We make lists for daily chores, short and long-term goals, special house remodeling projects, etc. Not only does this help our mental decluttering, but it promotes unity. Sharing and planning everything together, from our day off to our dreams, draws us closer and provides a tangible way to recognize our progress. We enjoy reasons to celebrate, so we utilize what we're doing as a chance to pat ourselves on the back.

Don't let mental clutter devour your ability to operate with confidence and success. Take a step back, declutter, organize, and watch your efficiency and joy surge.

Release the Catch

What have you caught along life's path that you would rather not have kept? Unlike fishing, where a decision is made almost immediately what to keep versus what to throw back, we regularly overlook the fact that we have a choice. We harbor items with hurtful memories, pictures with sad stories, and letters with cruel words. Think about your collection. Along with these effects, what about the ancient documents that we all hang onto. Mortgage papers from the house we owned three homes ago and checking account statements that are over a dozen years old. We could all swap stories and attempt to one-up each other with the undesirable and needless collections we've amassed.

[*Lindon*] I realized as soon as my divorce was final that I needed to remove these harmful and unnecessary items from my life. I lit up the fire pit in my backyard and over the course of a few evenings, methodically destroyed all of the negativity I could get my hands on. It was the most freeing and uplifting mental boost I could have possibly hoped for at that time in my life. There was no anger in my actions, yet present was the appreciation for a new beginning and an acknowledgement that the past belonged where the word suggests—in the past. I had no clue that less than a year later, I would be helping Sherry do the same thing.

Sherry's desk was one of the first targets of her initial decluttering effort. Her desk housed documents and letters that were over two decades old and paperwork from city, school, and divorce battles that were waged long ago. I was blown away that Sherry had held onto all this clutter, and I didn't waste any time encouraging her to get rid of it all.

Needless to say, I received almost the same reaction to this suggestion as I did to her bags that I told her to sell, sans the tears. At first Sherry was resistant, but it ended up being just as much a positive experience for her as it had been for me. I better let her explain this time around.

[*Sherry*] OK, so Lindon is quite right. I wasn't initially enthusiastic at his recommendation. See if you can relate to the following. The clutter I kept reminded me that I was right about my ex-husband and what a jerk he was. I had letters spouting vicious attacks in his handwriting, evidence for my righteous defense. And the documents from the city and school problems? I felt much the same about them: proof positive that I was right and others were wrong. Emails from the teacher in question that proved he was completely out of line and had unfairly condemned both my son and me. Contrary to how it may appear, I wasn't obsessed with the past, but on the occasion that I would ponder the hurt these people had inflicted, I felt secure and relieved possessing the evidence proving they were wrong—very wrong. Not terribly progressive, huh?

In hindsight, there are red flags all over the place with this rationale, but back then, it just felt good to hang on to all of it. Familiar. Comfortable. Safe. I felt protected and justified. Really, though, who was I ever going to show it to? Who would need to see it and what difference would it make? If I ever felt inclined to share what happened with someone, did I really need to shower them with concrete proof of my story or should my testimony have been enough? Instead of trusting God to provide for my needs, I defaulted to my worldly roots for an empty security. Clinging to the past was neither healthy nor progressive, and in direct opposition to what God calls us to do.

"'Jesus replied, No one who puts his hand to the plow and looks back is fit for service in the kingdom of God'" (Luke 9:62). This is straight from Jesus' mouth. We must abandon the past and focus the future on him.

"…Forgetting what is behind and straining toward what is ahead, I press on toward the goal to win the prize for which God has called me heavenward in Christ Jesus" (Phil. 3:13-14). Paul got it. He knew he needed to set aside anything that would distract him from being an effective Christian. Surely, what I had unknowingly been doing wasn't in line with God's directive for my life.

In addition to the personal justification collection, I too had my share of old, unneeded documents, including medical bills from the birth of my sons who are now young adults. How many times had I moved this paperwork with absolutely no reason to even keep it? Absurd! Lindon questioned me on why I was harboring these things and gave me solid reasons why it was advisable to let it all go. I knew he was right and it was time.

[*Lindon*] So Sherry put together a huge box of everything she could find, and we took it over to her sister's house. We sat in the driveway and spent hours burning each paper. For Sherry, it was cathartic and exhausting but, at the end of the night, she was free. Not only did she tell me so, but I could see it in her soot-covered face. She had cleansed scarred parts of her heart and freed her mind of considerable mental clutter. It was a tremendous step in the right direction. Painful memories may still remain, but they fade much more quickly when you're not constantly reminded of the heartache. Release, release, release. The freedom and healing you will experience is unparalleled.

Dis Discontentment

There is nothing that can inhibit us quite as much as feeling a lack of contentment. It's like a cancer that begins without an obvious cause or provocation. One seemingly unimportant dissatisfaction breeds another and then spreads like a dreaded disease into unrelated areas of our lives. Before we know it, our entire being is consumed with disappointment and frustration, and we might not even be able to remember how it all started.

Allowing this mindset will rob you of ever feeling total fulfillment and gratification. How can you when you're obsessed with what you don't have, where you don't live, what you can't buy, where you can't go, and what you can't do? The negativity in that thread of thinking is dark and foreboding and will bog your brain down and keep it there. The restlessness that comes from always wanting and looking for something better is exasperating, and the depression that ensues from never quite getting it all is life-altering. Emotional discord can have real physical consequences. "A heart at peace gives life to the body, but envy rots the bones" (Prov. 14:30).

We know someone who suffers from this condition. If she doesn't have it, she wants it. If she has it but you bought a better one, she must acquire the best to top the better. If, by chance, she doesn't have something and has no plans to get it, she feels compelled to explain why she doesn't intend to do so. It's almost as if she must announce her decision so you know it was an intentional choice on her part and not that it was out of her financial reach. This person, on the outside, has it all: a gorgeous home, financial stability, a healthy family, and lots of friends. It pains us to see her navigate this path. The money she spends trying to satiate her discontentment is exorbitant, and the toes she steps on along the way are numerous. We're exhausted just watching and listening, so we can't imagine how drained she personally feels. And for what? It just makes no sense.

Practicing an attitude of gratitude can make all the difference. Try replacing "I hope" for something you desire, as opposed to "I want." This removes the necessity from the desire and sets you up for less disappointment if the "I hope" doesn't come to fruition. Consider what you've done and acquired over the past year. What brought you true joy and what was honestly no more than a stepping stone to propel you forward in conquering the next "I want"? Develop a true appreciation for what you already have and realize that it's probably more than the majority of the world's population could ever hope to get a glimpse of. Delight in your blessings instead of always longing for more. Adjust your attitude of discontentment and meditate on the glass being half full, a simple analogy that is a powerful tool. Above all else, seek God for strength and guidance. Remember that everything you need and all you should want are in Christ Jesus anyway, so why look elsewhere? "But godliness with contentment is great gain. For we brought nothing into this world and we can take nothing out of it" (1 Tim. 6:6-7).

Hebrews 13: 5 drives the point home further. "Keep your lives free from the love of money and be content with what you have, because God has said, 'Never will I leave you; never will I forsake you.'" This verse is true for so much more than just money. We become content when we realize that God can and will meet all of our needs. Every last one! What are we searching for?

There are certainly times when even the most contented of us feel discontentment. That's life. It's unavoidable. We pray, though, that you'll have a heightened sense of awareness to this behavior so when it rears its head, you'll manage it swiftly and deter the breeding of frustration and despair. If you have God reigning in your life with the promise of eternal salvation, what you do or don't have on this earth becomes relatively insignificant.

Water off a Duck's Back

What else can you do, practically, to attain peace of mind? Decluttering the negative is a critical part of the process but, as with the other areas we've discussed, going a step further and putting aids in place to prevent future clutter from accumulating is just as vital.

The saying "water off a duck's back" provides a great analogy for what we recommend. Ducks have an oil-secreting gland that spreads oil over their feathers and gives them the ability to repel water. Much the same way water rolls off of a duck, you need to allow the small stuff to roll right off of you. There are times that it's healthy to let the big stuff go too! You must repel the negative if you don't want the potential for it to sink in. We're sure you've also heard, "in one ear and out the other." Same concept applies. There's no avoiding the fact that you'll be confronted with the undesirable, but what you do with it is your choice. If you allow it to permeate your being and fester within, you'll be consumed with the consequences. However, if you don't let the unwanted in, if you don't give it the slightest foothold, it can't take root and will shrivel and die. Good riddance!

Letting go of what you have no control over is another useful tool. How often do you try to manipulate situations which you have no "say so" over? Oh, but you want it to be a certain way. You know what's best. While these feelings may contain some truth, if it's not something within your control, or better yet, even if you can control it but it's not something you should be meddling in, it's time to take a step back.

[*Sherry*] Let me give you an example of a circumstance where letting go was essential. Decades ago I was in an undesirable financial spot. I was co-owner of a business that was failing and the bills were piling up. To top things off, I was seven months pregnant and stressed to the max. I worried about what would happen constantly. Bill collectors called incessantly, and I felt there was nowhere to hide from the harassment and shame. I allowed my weekends, my largest span of free time with Ryan, to be consumed and paralyzed by fear. I wasn't separating work from home, and this was prohibiting me from enjoying time with my precious two-year-old. A friend, who was aware of my struggle, posed a question. She asked if, while the banks were closed from Friday at 5 p.m. until Monday at 9 a.m., I had any ability to rectify the situation. Was anything going to drastically change financially with my business during the weekend hours? The absolute truth of the matter was a simple "no." Then why, she asked, was I wasting valuable time with my son worrying about something I had zero control over? That really made sense. She wasn't suggesting that I didn't have problems to resolve or that they were going to magically disappear, but the reality was that wasting time during the periods in which I couldn't possibly affect any change was the wrong choice. As soon as I understood the logic in her argument, I was sold. There was so much freedom in letting go, even if just for a weekend at a time. It gave me the chance to recharge and enjoy my son. I've applied this concept frequently since and it has always served me well. God bless her for her wise advice!

If you really want peace, follow that often-used adage: Let Go and Let God! Yes, the logic in my friend's argument made letting go easier in that situation, but the underlying lesson gave me the awareness I needed to rely on my faith walk in other situations where I needed to let go. Unclench your fingers and your mind will follow. Loosen your grip, turn it over to God, and experience the peace that results. Once you get the hang of it, there won't be any turning back.

How about ditching your "stinkin thinkin"? This is one of Lindon's friend's sayings. Negative thinking and a victim mentality can undermine and sabotage the best of us. You have to make a conscious choice to replace destructive thoughts with constructive ones. There's a learning experience in any situation, so seize it for all it's worth, and make it work for your benefit. If this is a stretch for you, seek out others for inspiration and example. Find those that have made good from bad and bathe in their stories of triumph. How did they overcome mental obstacles? The common thread will most assuredly be their positive mindset and determination. The Bible not only speaks of peace in the calm and tranquil sense, but also refers to having peace as being fearless, victorious, and triumphant. Soldier, let the negativity go and find your peace!

How Do You Heal?

We all have different ways of processing heartache and healing; what's revolutionary for one may be useless for another. We are prime examples of this. For me [Sherry] unraveling the reasons behind why something happened brings understanding, perspective, and promotes healing. It's much easier for me to deal with and accept what has transpired, whether I liked it or not, if I can figure out where it came from. I grew up with a strong desire to be in control. I sought it out and ran with it any chance I got. I didn't mind what responsibility it brought as long as I was holding the reins.

My parents divorced when I was quite young, and I rarely saw my dad. On one of his infrequent visits when I was about four or five years old, he came to see me while I was at his parents' condo. I remember standing on the seventh floor balcony, crying inconsolably, while I watched him walking away down on the street. I can even remember him turning around and walking backwards while he waved to me. I yelled for him to promise to come back, but inside I knew I wouldn't see him for a long time. My Nana kept trying to get me back inside, but it was to no avail. I'm sure it was heartbreaking for her to witness. It tugs at my heart, even today, when I relive this moment. It brings up painful memories of feeling utterly helpless. I had no control over the situation, yet it was dictating so much to me. Even at that tender young age I knew I didn't like that one bit! It wasn't until about six years ago that I connected that exact moment as being one that profoundly influenced my lifelong control issues. The instant I did, however, I was able to methodically process through my feelings. It was amazing how quickly I was able to make significant, positive changes that seemed far out of reach just moments before.

[*Lindon*] For me it's more about just finding true forgiveness and forgetfulness, no matter what the circumstance, and moving forward without looking back. I don't necessarily need to know exactly what prompted a particular occurrence or situation. I don't mind discussing it with Sherry and working through it, but my heart is restored when I simply lay my burdens at Jesus' feet and allow him to do a work of healing in my heart. At one of the lowest points in my life, I simply walked and prayed, and mixed in a bit of crying, every day for six months. The situation was something I just couldn't comprehend, and I knew better than to beat myself up trying to figure it out. There was no rational answer for what had been going on and no way to explain it away. For me, to analyze and dissect the components over and over would have continually dredged up the pain of it all. Even my counselor told me to not ask *why* because there was no answer that would make sense or soothe me. I begged God to deliver and protect me from having a hard heart, and he provided in a mighty and profound way. Praise God for his unending faithfulness and grace! So for me, I just hand it over to God, dive in the Word, lose myself in worship, and make a choice to walk in his light. I'm determined to do the best I can in each situation, regardless of the history.

How do you heal? Think about times in your past when you were able to overcome a negative emotion or situation. What did it take to get the job done? We've shared just two of our experiences, but there are as many paths to healing as there are problems to overcome. Working through it is a personal journey and not necessarily one that you should go through alone. Sometimes it's helpful to talk to people you know and trust as they may have insight that you wouldn't have thought of on your own. Depending on the severity of the problem, you may need to go a step further and consider other avenues of help such as those suggested in the introduction to this book. We firmly believe in the advice we offer, but it's no substitute for specialized expert help when warranted. If you are suffering from deep emotional, physical, or spiritual wounding, please seek the help of a licensed professional.

Regardless of what route you take toward healing, just be sure you invest the effort to make it happen. Just as a long distance runner wouldn't expect to be able to run a marathon on a broken leg, you can't run your life race with a broken heart or mind. Both must repair, heal, train, and find the path of success to the finish line.

The Lies We Are Led to Believe

What if you read this chapter and, while you think it sounds fairly logical and rational, you're too caught up in your old ways to change? What if you don't have the strength to make the changes you desire? Perhaps you are in such denial that you can't even recognize that you're a considerable distance from where you ought to be?

What do you do if you've isolated yourself from family and friends because you don't want their advice or input, even though you may know you need it? Have you become unapproachable? What if you are drowning in a sea of loneliness, despair, shame, misery, grief, or anger? Are you angry at God for a season in your life where you felt he abandoned you? Could you be running from a hurtful situation that you have no idea how to handle? How in the world do you pull yourself out of something that you may not understand is detrimental? You must see things for what they are so you can pull the trigger of action and start making them right, but it's a catch-22. What if you can't even recognize it to begin with? What if you're so consumed with mind clutter that you can't see outside the mess? Don't despair! You are not alone and there is a solution.

Take heart because this is exactly where the Holy Spirit shines and runs to your aid. You aren't built to rely solely on your own strength or perspective. Yes, God gave you a brain and he expects you to use it, but he is also well aware that in your humanity, you are broken and cannot go this alone. This is why he provides the Holy Spirit to love you and show you the way. You are never, ever alone! Enlist the Spirit's help. He's your ace in the hole. When you are unable to see things for what they are, the Holy Spirit will reveal to you all that you need.

You see, Satan attempts to snare all of us. He tells us lie after lie to trap us, keep us down, and bind us up in the failures of our past. He encourages us to wallow in self-pity and tells us we're strong for casting aside anyone who has caused us pain. He wants us to believe that we can't trust anyone or that we aren't worth anything. The devil wants us isolated and removed because then we are easy pickings. An

216 | *Declutter Now!*

old pastor friend of Lindon's calls it "devil bait." He sets us up to reel us in.

Whether you think you're an easy target or not, pray this prayer just in case, and ask the Holy Spirit to do miraculous works in your life:

"God, I come before you and ask you to reveal the clutter in my mind and heart. Make my roadblocks known to me, and open my eyes so that I may see things clearly. Give me the motivation and strength to conquer and declutter all that stands in the way of my joy and service to you. Show me all that I must do, to be all you long for me to be. Cast away any lies I've been told, set me free from the bondage of my past, and send it all straight back to the pit of hell. Heavenly Father, allow me to see whatever I must, and set me free from the controlling spirit of deceit. Please enter into this situation and take control. Heal me, guide me, direct me, and soften my heart so I will embrace your work in my life. I love you and I thank you for all that you are about to do. Amen."

As you read the prayer, didn't it feel good just to say it? To hand your concerns and requests over to someone you trust who can actually do something about it? It does for us! This is a catch-all and if you pray this or something similar to it often, it will keep you open to the Holy Spirit's help. Listen and become sensitive to what God is showing you. Expect that God will work miracles in your life. As your challenges are revealed by the Holy Spirit, begin including them in your prayers. For instance:

"I am stubborn, set in my ways, and often can't see outside of my own thoughts."

"I have shut out family and friends who have been honest and well meaning."

"I am lost in my pain and anger over past hurts."

Whatever the case may be, BRING IT! There isn't anything the Holy Spirit hasn't heard before, and he knows just what to do with your concerns, in fact, he's waiting for you to approach him right now. Don't delay!

God Matters

If you can be sure of nothing else, if you are uncertain what advice to take, what to pitch, and what to make a priority, know this: God matters! If you figure this out and make the effort to place him in his rightful spot, the rest will fall into place. Remember, the purpose behind all that we're saying and doing is to declutter the distractions and destructions in your life so you arrive at a place where you have the freedom to choose him! That's what melts God's heart.

The only way God's plan would work was if he granted us the ability to have free will, so he did. We get to choose—we pick. Of course he wants us to choose him, but he won't force us to do so! We're praying not only that you choose him, but that your life is free from emotional bondage so you can enjoy serving him in a way that glorifies his name to the fullest and brings you uncontainable joy.

God wants to deliver you from all that ails you. He wants you free to serve him with your whole heart. He wants all of you and will do anything he can to ensure you are in a position to do this, but you have to do your part. Ask the Holy Spirit in and allow his work to be done in your life. If you have shut him out, bring him back. If you have had God on the back burner, time to move him up! All is never lost. Thank goodness God allows U-turns. Pray. Change your direction. Our goal is to guide and direct you right into the loving arms of your Lord and Savior, Jesus Christ.

Set your mind on what really matters. The positive life changes and ongoing benefits will convince you that you're on the right path. Life is too short (or long) to be cluttered, unhappy, chasing the unsatisfying, and wasting time consumed by negative emotions, thoughts, and actions. Don't settle or sell yourself short. Invite the Holy Spirit in and start living a life filled with incomparable peace and joy. What have you got to lose? All that doesn't matter, that's what!

Chapter 8

Soul Searching—DECLUTTER & *GO*!

HELLOOOOOO GOD. COME OUT, COME out wherever you are! Peek-a-boo, I need to see you!

Have you had a hard time finding God lately? Has it been a while? At times it may seem as though God is absent, but it's never God hiding from you, rather God being hidden in the clutter of your life. It's an epic problem and most people, even Christians, desperately need a good game of "God Seek" from time to time. We're prayerful that the first seven chapters have provided insight on exactly how to make space in your life for God. That's what it's all about, isn't it? At the end of the day, it's about putting God first, proactively loving him, and appreciating all that he did for us.

"[B]ut God demonstrates his own love for us in this: while we were still sinners, Christ died for us" (Rom. 5:8). You might have heard that verse a dozen times or perhaps never before, but take a moment and think about the weight of the message in these few words. God wasn't rewarding us for being good or beaming with pride at our perfection. Not even close. While we were still sinners, WHILE we were misbehaving and completely flawed in nature and character, God made the ultimate sacrifice and sent his beloved son to suffer on our behalf and redeem us because he loved us so very much. Awesome, isn't it? Doesn't that cause you to pause in utter amazement? Could you do that? To be honest, we have a hard time sacrificing for those who seem undeserving. Heck, sometimes we have a hard time sacrificing at all.

The truth is that while you *owe* God your life, he doesn't want your heart out of guilt or fear. He longs for you to desire a relationship with him: to love, honor, and serve him. He allows free will for this very reason. He gives you the choice. And that's what it's all about, folks, choosing to declutter each area of your life, the life that Christ gave you to begin with, so you have the freedom, energy, and time to choose God.

Perhaps you've never sought God but are feeling convicted and moved that this is the time to start. All you need is the desire and motivation and he's there for the asking. Whether this is new to you, or you're a longtime believer excited to rid your life of the clutter and enjoy a deeper, more meaningful relationship with Christ, this chapter's for you.

Comprehensive Culmination

In each of the previous chapters, we've been coaching on how to declutter different areas of your life. The effects of this process are far reaching and go well beyond the desk that got cleaned off, the budget that was created, and the reevaluation of the kids' activity schedule. Decluttering as a whole is beneficial to you personally as a wife, a husband, a mother, a father, a friend, etc., but also, even more importantly, as a child of God. The culmination of this declutter, the most important end result, the big crescendo, is that you'll have more time and freedom for God. You should have less in your life of what doesn't matter, so you have the ability to make room for what does. Remember, less is more! If you truly have a heart for God and want to enter in with him, spread his light, and do good works on his behalf, decluttering will give you the resources you need to make this to happen.

There comes a time to stop thinking about things and start doing them and, in this case, when you do so, you have a failsafe assurance. If you desire a relationship with God, the chance of this coming to fruition is 100%. There is no gambling or risk involved. IF you make the choice, it WILL happen. All of what you want is available simply for the asking. When you prepare and pave the way to make this a reality, it WILL become so. How many things in life are guaranteed? Aside from the fact that Lindon's used floss will never, ever, land completely inside the bathroom wastebasket, and one day your physical existence on this earth will cease, nothing else is certain, except for the availability of a relationship with Jesus Christ.

God Space

Do you have room in your life for God? Just like the end result of cleaning out a messy closet or drawer, have you now made enough space in your daily routine, and in your heart and mind, for God to have a place to dwell? He deserves so much more than just the leftovers, the fractions of fleeting seconds available between the rush of activity, or the fluke moments where, by chance, there is some time for him. Where there is no intentionality, there is often no success. Stop accepting that method as good enough or the best you've got right now. You get God's best; he puts you first. Shouldn't you afford God the same standing in your life?

Declutter & *Go*

Let's say you've decluttered and made room in your life to commune with God, then what? First, pat yourself on the back for a job well done. It's not easy to change old habits and routines, even when they aren't good for you, and perfectly okay to pause for a moment and reflect on how far you've come. We're seriously proud of you for taking our advice to heart and giving it a try. What to do next? So many people get tripped up at this point, and we don't want you to become one of them.

This is where you GO! You must use this extra time and space to do what God desires for your life and act on what your heart yearns for so desperately. A great idea will forever stay just that, only an idea, unless you put action behind it. Even when decluttered, we can still become complacent and stall, that's why this is a two-step process. You must DECLUTTER & GO! We aren't living in a dress rehearsal and every minute that ticks by is lost forever. God paid a price for our time and freedom, a price greater than anything we can wrap our minds around. We're pretty sure he didn't do this for us to abuse the privileges he provided. Don't waste your time and don't waste his. *Do* the things you feel called to do, put action behind your desires, and go after them.

Galvanizing the *Go*

So, how do you GO? How do you physically and emotionally bring God back to front and center in your daily life, or maybe give him top billing for the first time ever? Red Rover, Red Rover, it's time to bring God right over. There are so many meaningful ways to reach out and draw him close. We aren't referring to acting religious, a trap many people get caught in to *look* or *feel* Christian. We're talking about opening your heart and mind and allowing him, today, to use all you for his kingdom and glory.

Jesus said, "Come follow me." To those called, he didn't suggest to come back when they were done with other things and make time for him then. Jesus meant NOW, and the men that followed him knew it. They obeyed by serving with their whole hearts and were instantly transformed and called disciples. Those that didn't, and there were many, had too much stuff, too much clutter, to be available for Jesus. Can you imagine how they were kicking themselves after the fact, when the evidence was irrefutable that Jesus was Lord? Unlike those men, you already have proof of this guarantee; you have it right now. How can you possibly say no?

Use as Needed

No matter how busy or lazy we are, it's amazing how quickly we find God when we need him. When we're facing insurmountable odds or going through a challenging time, we seek him out immediately. We step up the pace a notch or two, or ten, to get to him as fast as humanly possible. Truthfully, God wants us to seek him out during tough times, but there's so much joy and blessing to be had when we obediently place him in the center of our lives, right in the middle of "Ring around the Rosie," when life is going along just fine. Think about the fire that is lit under our tootsies when we want or need something badly, and then purposefully incorporate that type of energy and zeal into seeking God on a daily basis. That's the passion we need to bring into our walk with God every day.

Jumpstart

Let's say you believe Jesus Christ to be your Lord and Savior. You've confessed this to God and are ready to embark on your path. Perhaps, you've known Jesus for a good portion of your life but never entered into a relationship with him. What if you had a great connection with God but, for one reason or another, it fizzled out. Regardless of your history, how do you jumpstart your relationship with God now? As you start experiencing him in your life, you'll develop your own personal rapport and groove, but to get you started, we'd like to share some of our favorite ways we enjoy spending time with God.

Prayer Priority

A deep and genuine prayer life is foundational in getting and staying close to God. It's one-on-one time with your Father when you can have a personal audience and don't even have to share. He's all yours! Anytime. Anywhere. Mornings, evenings, during drive times, while taking a neighborhood stroll, in the midst of daily devotions… It's your opportunity to speak freely and bring any concerns and heartaches to his attention. You can thank him for all that he's done and will do in your life. It can be a time of reflection, questions, praises, and relationship building. You can lay everything at God's feet; nothing will scare him off. You can approach him with full confidence that he'll never, ever turn you away. Who else gives you this unconditional love and acceptance? Who else can offer you the guarantees that God extends? It's an offer you shouldn't pass up, and all you have to do is talk to God.

When laying your heart before the Lord, when you enter his glorious presence, approach him with a reverent and humble spirit. Even while conveying your earthly desires, seek his response first for your life.

James tells us, "Humble yourselves before the Lord, and he will lift you up"(4:10). This was from Jesus' own brother. We don't know too many people that would instruct you to treat their sibling in this manner unless they truly meant business. James was a loyal servant of Christ and a leader of the church in Jerusalem. He lived what he preached and he knew his brother was the real deal.

In 2 Chronicles 7:14, the Lord himself coaches us in our interaction with him and says, "'if my people, who are called by my name, will humble themselves and pray and seek my face and turn from their wicked ways, then I will hear from heaven and will forgive their sin and will heal their land.'" He is always acting on your behalf, and you can trust that he knows exactly what's best for you. Lift up your petitions to God, but do it with the respect that he deserves, and with the confidence of God's infinite wisdom and unfailing love for you. A consistent and meaningful prayer life is the best first step in building your relationship with Christ. Make an effort to carve out daily time with him and your return will be tenfold.

Learning to Listen

An area that often gets overlooked is the opposite of your prayer life. Instead of talking to God, be sure you stop and spend quality time listening. I [Sherry] heard a sermon some years back that really spoke to my heart. The pastor was urging the congregation to stop and listen to God. He suggested that while a prayer life is extremely important, it's just as vital to balance out speaking with a healthy dose of listening. Sounds pretty rudimentary, doesn't it? Think about it though. For most of us, the talking comes a whole lot easier and much more naturally than the listening. This is certainly the case for Lindon and me. We are both big (BIG) talkers and work diligently at good listening skills to ensure we are courteous in our exchange. The last thing we want is for the other to feel bored, mowed over, or otherwise disenchanted with our conversation.

Isn't this true of all our dialogues? If we aren't good listeners, we run the risk of offending people by making them feel unimportant, and losing their attention by boring them to tears. Who wants to listen to someone so self-absorbed that they are more interested in hearing themselves speak than engaging in meaningful discussion? Have you had relationships where this was a predominant theme? If so, aren't these the same people that, over time, you began avoiding? Who wants to sit there and be dictated to? It just gets old and irritating.

It's much the same with God. While God doesn't get bored hearing us talk or ticked off because he can't get a word in edgewise, he does desire us to take a break from speaking and listen to what he's got to say. God doesn't waste his words or time, and always has our best interests in mind. We can rest assured that if he takes the time to speak to us, it's significant and worth listening to. In the clutter of our loud and demanding lives, we often get so lost in the talking that we don't close our mouths long enough to hear a thing. How can God speak to us, answer our questions, and care for our hearts if we don't pause to hear his voice and embrace his wisdom? How can we take direction and obtain his counsel if we aren't available to receive what he's got to say. Simply put, we can't, and what a loss this is. As Lindon says, there's a reason we have one mouth and two ears!

Holy Spirit 101

Before we move on, just a little footnote on how God speaks to us. We could write an entire book on the Holy Spirit alone, but for the sake of broaching the subject and providing some basics, we're going to give you a little tease. For some, this may be old hat but for others, this may be something you're hearing for the first time; you might even be a little unnerved by it all. Not to worry! Just take it in and ask God to share with you the truths he wants you to know. Welcome to Holy Spirit 101.

God, our Heavenly Father, almighty Creator of heaven and earth, and Master of the universe doesn't work alone. Say what? Seriously? Yup, seriously! He is actually three divine persons wrapped into one. The Trinity refers to God the Father, God the Son (Jesus), and God the Holy Spirit, sometimes referred to as the Holy Ghost. God the Father is the most recognizable and familiar of the triune. Most people even understand Jesus to be God's son, though they may not realize that Jesus co-exists with God, having exactly the same nature and attributes as God. They often don't realize the same is true for the Holy Spirit. This is difficult to wrap your mind around, so here's an analogy that we find helpful. Consider H2O. The combination of elements designated as H2O can form a liquid (water), a gas (steam), or a solid (ice), but regardless of which form it's in, it still encompasses the same elements. This is a way to think of the Trinity. While God the Father, Jesus, and the Holy Spirit are separate entities, they are all made up of the same characteristics and qualities, and work in unison with one another.

"For God so loved the world that he gave his one and only Son, that whoever believes in him shall not perish but have eternal life" (John 3:16). Most people are familiar with this verse. In fact, even non-believers can often recite the words from just having heard it repeatedly over the

228 | *Declutter Now!*

course of their lives. Jesus is out there. However, how many of you have heard the following verses?

"But the Counselor, the Holy Spirit, whom the Father will send in my name, will teach you all things and will remind you of everything I have said to you" (John 14:26) (The Holy Spirit is of God.)

"Therefore go and make disciples of all nations, baptizing them in the name of the Father and of the Son and of the Holy Spirit" (Mt. 28:19). (Evidence of the Trinity.)

Peter replied, "Repent and be baptized, every one of you, in the name of Jesus Christ for the forgiveness of your sins. And you will receive the gift of the Holy Spirit" (Acts 2:38). (Assurance the Holy Spirit is yours by profession of faith.)

The Holy Spirit definitely doesn't get the billing Jesus does! How can we be so sure that the Holy Spirit is actually God? The Bible speaks clearly to this point. One passage in Acts 5:3-4 directly links God and the Holy Spirit as one. Peter was chastising Ananias for lying to the Holy Spirit and then in the same breath said that Ananias didn't lie to *men but to God*, thus indicating the Holy Spirit and God are *one and the same*.

Paul writes in First Corinthians 2:11 that no one knows the thoughts of God except the Spirit of God. The Spirit is God. The Holy Spirit is mentioned and present in both the Old and New Testament. Jesus teaches on the Holy Spirit and countless others mention him as well, but yet the Holy Spirit is often overlooked and misunderstood. Without a doubt, he's the least conspicuous of the three.

Even though we're keeping it light, we want to leave you with more than just this basic characterization, so let's delve just a bit further and expand on what the Holy Spirit does and how he goes about doing it.

We believe the Holy Spirit is the voice of God. He's the nudge that tells you to do something when you hadn't thought of it on your own. The intuition that warns you of danger or helps you find something lost. It's that feeling you get when you know God is speaking to you. When you have moments of instinct, clarity, vision, and awareness, it's often the Holy Spirit at work in your life. Have you ever told a story and used the line "and it occurred to me..." or "in that moment I just knew...." That is likely God coming to you in the form of the Holy Spirit. It's the sixth sense or insight you have, or that hunch you pat yourself on the back for while marveling at how you came up with it on your own. Well, we don't want to burst your bubble, but often the credit should go to the Holy Spirit.

It's fascinating that we all hear from the Holy Spirit in different ways and at different times. There's no set method that he uses to communicate with us. It may be when entering into prayer or worship, during a dream, or perhaps when finally slowing down and resting at the end of a long day. For me [*Sherry*] it always seems to be when I am doing my hair in the morning. Talk about odd timing! Whatever the case may be, the Holy Spirit is always there and definitely not shy. I love reflecting on my personal Holy Spirit stories because they remind me how very real God is and allow me to bask in the confidence of his presence. Allow me to share one of my favorites.

Holy Spirit Unplugged

My aunt passed away in February 2001. She was the kind of aunt you loved to death but one who could also drive you crazy. She could be difficult to deal with, and that's putting it mildly. Right before Christmas 2001 she said a few things that really rubbed me the wrong way. Consequently, I returned the picture frame I bought her for Christmas. I realize I was being a bit spiteful, but she had really irritated me! On her deathbed, I whispered in her ear that I was sorry for having been angry with her, even though I don't think she even knew I had been. She certainly didn't know I had returned her gift, but I did and I felt bad.

I went to the store to purchase the original frame again, thinking that it would be the perfect parting gift to place in her casket. The store was sold out of the exact one I'd previously purchased and I was heartbroken. I went to another store close by but the story was the same. I even called a few more in the area, but it was to no avail. I was sitting in my living room the night before the funeral, contemplating what to get my aunt, when the Holy Spirit said to me, "Look down by your leg, Sherry." It wasn't an audible voice but one I heard in my head and heart. It caught me a little off guard and struck me as a bit bizarre but, of course, I looked. Next to my leg, between the chair and the wall, was a wrapped Christmas present. I knew instantly what God was saying to me.

I completely forgot that months before, I had actually bought two of the same frames, one for my aunt and one for another friend. I hadn't seen my other friend since Christmas, so there her frame sat, still wrapped and ready to go. I'm not sure I can really explain the joy I felt deep in my heart. Not only did I now have the EXACT frame I wanted to give to my aunt, but I had the Holy Spirit speaking to me personally and caring for me so lovingly. It was a moment of reassurance I will never, ever forget.

Plugging In

So how do you plug in to the Holy Spirit? How does he enter into your life? When you accept Jesus Christ as your personal Lord and Savior, the Holy Spirit is part of the package. His presence and spiritual breath will fill you up and permeate your heart and soul. He'll always be there for you and will never forsake you or fail you, just like the God he is.

In hindsight, you may realize now that something you thought was just intuition was actually the Holy Spirit speaking to you. In the future, your awareness will be more acute since you now have a better idea what you're looking for. The goal is to train yourself to hear God. To listen for him and heed his will for your life is one of the greatest gifts you can give yourself. Quiet down and make yourself available and accessible to him. Incredible things happen when you start acknowledging and experiencing the Holy Spirit in your life. Give it a try!

Social Selection

The next suggestion goes hand and hand with much of the information presented in the chapter on relationships. When you are choosing with whom to spend time, make an effort to enjoy the company of those friends and family members who will encourage your walk with God. How comfortable is it when you can sit down and talk to someone freely and have the confidence of knowing they can relate to the core values of your belief system? We each have friends who come from a wide variety of backgrounds, from every end of the spectrum you can imagine. Many are Christians but there are a lot of unbelievers as well. We love each person dearly and glean something special from every relationship or we wouldn't sustain it, but there is also no denying there's something unique about spending time with brothers and sisters in Christ. These are, or should be, the friends that will hold you accountable in your Christian walk and those you can rely on for spiritual encouragement and guidance. God calls us to gather and two or more qualify!

Do you have friends that operate like chameleons—their attitudes and language change with their surroundings? Have you ever noticed even your own actions vary depending on whose company you're in? On occasion, we've been guilty of the same. Knowing this, doesn't it just make sense to surround yourself with those whose mere presence influences you to stay true to your Christian self? It often takes more effort to make the better choice but, in the long run and in terms of eternity, which will bring you the pay off? Use good sense and keep yourself in the right situations with the right people. Don't overlook the impact your social environment has on your spiritual life.

Word Consumption

Do you enjoy reading Christian material and listening to music by Christian artists? For reading, the Bible is a great place to start, but if you haven't been to a Christian bookstore lately, you're long overdue and really missing out. There are enough fiction and non-fiction books to satisfy any interest and speak to every genre imaginable. Especially with Christian books, you want to be certain the author is credible, but if you start with some solid recommendations or pick the brains of the bookstore employees, you should get off on the right foot.

As with books, music is available to suit every taste. As a friend told us, it's not the music that's Christian but the words. So true! Are you a fan of country, top 40, old time rock and roll, hip hop, or even the current scream-o sensation (not us!)? It's all available. Surround yourself with words that soothe, inspire, encourage, and motivate. Listen to Christian radio and never again worry what might be said that would cause you to cringe for fear your kids are listening. It's quite liberating! So whether your passion is reading, music, or both, give the Christian element a try. It's a great way to effortlessly infuse more of God into your daily life.

"Those who live according to the sinful nature have their minds on what that nature desires; but those who live in accordance with the Spirit have their minds set on what the Spirit desires" (Rom. 8:5). God makes it crystal clear what we are to surround ourselves with and why. You know the old saying, "you are what you eat"? While that may be referring to the food you ingest, it also holds true for the other things you consume as well. You are what you read, what you listen to, what you absorb and retain, and what you allow to dwell within you. It all counts and makes a cumulative impact on your soul.

The Case for Church

This brings us to the next integral part of a well-balanced walk with Christ. Statistics show time and time again that believers who attend church regularly and actively live out their faith live longer lives, recover from illness more quickly, succumb to divorce less, have more energy, feel more hope and are, in general, happier people. Doesn't this list make you want to grab a piece of the action?

The church, as most people recognize it, is a physical structure, the place where believers gather with other believers to worship and get fed spiritually. The Bible also refers to the church as the body of Christ, the body of believers themselves. The discussion in this chapter is going to focus on the actual church you attend. Understand that, for a Christian, the church IS you and is always within you. You need only look in your heart and soul to find God and all he encompasses.

There are as many different viewpoints about organized religion and attending church as there are churches to pick from, and we aren't going to debate all the ins and outs. If you have any misgivings or negative, pre-conceived notions, we recommend you read what the Bible says on the matter and pray for God's direction and guidance. We believe the church to be an instrumental part of our walk, and we strongly encourage you to make it a part of yours. Our experiences have taught us much along the way, and we pray the truths we share in the next few sections will aid you in making the right choices for you and your family.

Discerning the Differences

First and foremost, be certain the doctrine of the church you are visiting or attending supports your spiritual beliefs. There are an abundance of churches to choose from, with a surprisingly wide variation of doctrinal beliefs from church to church and, even more surprisingly, within the same denomination. It may seem odd to compare churches and select which one works best for you, almost like you're choosing your religion, but in a sense, you are. It's not a free for all, though! Our recommendation is to make sure, first and foremost, that it's a Bible-believing church with a Bible-teaching pastor.

The doctrine of the church should be thoroughly supported by Scripture. Spend time reading the Scripture quoted and see if you are comfortable with the church's interpretation. This is really key. You don't have to be a biblical scholar to have an educated opinion on what is accurate and comfortable to you. When reading verses, pray for God's truth to be shown to you. Reference a reputable study Bible and read the cliff notes version of the text. If something sounds fishy, you'll know it. And just to point out the obvious, interpreting Scripture is far different than making Scripture up, which of course isn't advisable or acceptable for any church or pastor to do. In fact, God specifically warns us against this in Revelation 22:18-19: "I warn everyone who hears the words of the prophecy of this book: If anyone adds anything to them, God will add him to the plagues described in this book. And if anyone takes words away from this book of prophecy, God will take away from him his share in the tree of life and in the holy city, which are described in this book."

Admittedly, some verses in the Bible are easier to understand than others, but this is one of the easy ones. Don't add or subtract from the words God has given or there will be dire consequences. Very simple. Very straightforward.

What is the church's position on salvation, the Trinity, hell, heaven, baptism, tithing, membership, etc.? The differences on positions will probably blow you away! We're all reading the same Bible, right? Sometimes it just doesn't seem so. Chances are you might never agree with everything, and that's to be expected, but don't compromise on the big stuff, and don't let the less significant things hold you back. It's an important personal choice, so give this decision the evaluation it deserves.

The church of today is considerably different than the church of the past. There are a wider variety of programs available that are sure to suit just about every passion, need, desire, or interest you might have. In some of the larger, mega-churches, you'll find up to five or six services a weekend, each with their own style and flavor of worship. They have classes for infants all the way up to senior citizens, activities for every holiday and occasion, and special events that will knock your socks off. We even have a local church in Phoenix that puts on an extravagant Christmas nativity show incorporating flying angels, pyrotechnics, live animals (camels included), and a forty-foot "singing tree" made up of choir members. The sky's the limit nowadays.

But, bigger isn't always better and more doesn't necessarily equate to quality. We've found churches that are so consumed with the entertainment factor that worship feels more like a concert performance than an intimate time to enter in with God. Some pastors are so worried about increasing attendance numbers that they offer flashy, hollow services to attract parishioners, but often sacrifice deep, meaningful worship time.

Speaking of Pastors...

And speaking of pastors, it's just as important to evaluate them as well as the church you're trying out. This may sound harsh and judgmental, but focus on the intention behind the action. Your spiritual walk is one of the most important aspects of your Christian life, and you can't be too careful in getting it right. Trust us, a pastor that's worth his salt is praying you get it right too and would wholly support your efforts and due diligence in checking him out.

Pastors come in every shape, size, and flavor imaginable. You can have the most genuine, faithful, educated pastor, but if he puts you to sleep in the pews, what impact will he have? Subliminal messaging isn't going to cut it here. What if the pastor focuses on life areas or stages that aren't of particular interest to you? What if the pastor is just too much of a "feel good" person and isn't willing to take a hard enough stand on issues you are passionate about, or worse, on any issues at all? Perhaps the pastor crosses lines when preaching that you don't feel are appropriate. Even pastors from the same denomination or affiliation can have different personalities, presentation styles, and hang-ups. Remember, pastors are people too! How often does the pastor teach? Who are his substitutes? Does he prefer teaching in a series style or by books of the Bible? Does he (or another staff member) do counseling? How involved is he in church activities? Is he spread too thin? What resources does he provide at the church for help when help is needed? Are you beginning to see how many variables there are and how crucial it is to be careful about what you commit yourself and your family to?

So yes, we're encouraging you to pursue a healthy and positive church life, but we've also inundated you with a variety of concerns and pitfalls. The point is that just because it's a church doesn't mean it's the right one for you. The name "church" doesn't insinuate that you should run with blind faith and present a blank check of your heart, time, and resources. Churches are imperfect because they are made up of imperfect people, and this includes the pastors too. The only perfect one to walk the earth was Jesus, so unless he's personally preaching, do your research and improve your chances exponentially of finding a church with a pastor you love that's a great fit for your family.

Don't Stop Short

Once the church and pastor pass your initial evaluations, take one more step before getting involved and drawn in. Take an inventory of what's most essential to you and consider what you intend to glean from your church life. Will the church fit your needs and desires? Do they offer programs for your children? Women's / Men's Bible studies, dinners, retreats, etc? Special events during the holidays? Are you interested in missions work? If so, make sure they're involved in supporting and promoting mission projects that touch your heart. How are they on community outreach? Would you like to sing or play in the worship band? Follow through in making sure you get what you're aiming for. With all there is to choose from, "your" church is likely out there, you just need to find it. And if, by chance, you find a church you love and it has most, but not all, of what you're looking for, maybe you can initiate and coordinate bringing other programs or services to the campus? If you're in the right spot, they will be appreciative of your offer. Most churches are grateful for new faces and helping hands.

No Isn't a Dirty Word

It's entirely possible to get just as cluttered and overwhelmed with church involvement as it is in other parts of your life. It's not "un-Christian" to evaluate the potential time commitment, benefit, and purpose, just as you would with any other activity. Know what you're willing to do and know when to say no. We've seen scores of people fall into this predicament. They allow themselves to get cluttered by church because they feel obligated to serve, to help, and to be obedient to God. Don't' fall into this trap. Your intent may be completely innocent and honorable, but if you're not careful, the end result can be just as destructive as clutter in any other area of your life will produce.

What we've also witnessed, and even been party to, is just with school and sports groups, it's the same few people who always step up and help. Do what you can and what's reasonable. There's definitely a time and place to be involved and you are called to do so, but make sure it's of your and God's choosing. It's all about burning on, not burning out. Keeping a healthy balance in everything you do will allow you to be effective and enjoy helping all the more. We simply can't stress this enough. If you get overcommitted, your time with Christ will ultimately suffer, and wouldn't that completely undermine what you were trying to accomplish when attending church in the first place?

Check Yourself

Interestingly, church can also be a source of creating unadulterated pride. Check yourself and make sure you're involved for the right reasons.

It's easy to be put on a pedestal by those you're helping, and that recognition will fuel your commitment to do more and more, potentially for the wrong reasons. We've both seen many a member of the worship team allow their pride to consume their being. Being on stage offers a sense of celebrity and garners much attention. Yup, even in church, arrogance can abound. Always remember the purpose of your involvement and make a conscientious decision to check the spirit behind your contribution. Remember when we discussed approaching God with a humble spirit? Well, this attitude is important to God in all that you do.

No Mixed Signals

It may sound like we're giving you mixed signals. Look for this but be careful of that. Do this but avoid that. By no means are we trying to confuse you or make this difficult. We simply want to guide you in the right direction while pointing out some concerns and challenges you may face. We know you're going to have to learn a lot of this for yourself but, like concerned and loving parents, we want to fully equip you and set you up for the best chance of success. We really do care.

Hopefully we've given you some ideas that will be useful in jump-starting or reigniting your walk. Of course, there are countless other ways to spend time with God, so be creative and don't pass on any positive opportunities to tap into your personal relationship with him.

Distractions and Decisions

So here you have it. Our solution to being cluttered and complacent is to DECLUTTER & GO! We've given you our best advice on decluttering every area of your life and some great ideas to get you going in your walk with Christ, but there is one more piece of the puzzle that'll

240 | **Declutter Now!**

round out the picture. Be on guard against distractions. Yes, we know, here we go again. Do this but be careful of that. We must have driven our kids crazy, in fact, we probably still do! The reality is, though, that distractions of every kind should be a real cause for concern. All the positive changes in your life are going to quickly get Satan's attention. It's tremendously easy to get sidetracked, especially when first starting on your journey, so be aware and stay the course. Satan is creative and cunning in how he'll try to trip you up, and if you're aware of this from the beginning, you'll have a better chance to catch it quickly, see it for what it is, and combat it effectively.

We've accomplished much on the decluttering side of things and are more than adequately active in the GO category, but we're also well aware that distractions come easy. Some are intentionally slung our way and others are just par for the course when living life. If we have one area where we have to try a little harder to walk our talk, this would be it. We make an intentional daily effort to avoid and battle diversions, but it takes a whole lot of work and attention to be successful. We discuss and carefully consider where we are in our walk and where we want to be. Equally as important is our commitment to thoroughly vet any decisions we are considering and to hold each other accountable for sticking to our plan and our priorities so we don't lose focus. We are just as capable as anyone else of squeezing God out, not only with things that should be decluttered, but with distractions that get us sidetracked. And think about it, distractions are not always obviously *bad*, but can appear to be of the good persuasion as well. Sometimes, even too much of a good thing ain't so good!

The truth is, though, that even if you spend time cleaning out each area of your life, not everything will fit into a nice neat category or box, and you should plan on expecting the unexpected. Even if you have a great *GO* plan and are successfully implementing it, you will be faced with decisions over and over again that have the potential to upset the apple cart. Things that didn't get addressed will rear their heads. New situations or opportunities will happen. It's in these types of choices that we really find out how much we've learned and what we're truly willing to do in order to achieve the desired end result. How you address and handle these occurrences will either reinforce all you've done and add to your success or derail it completely.

The "No Agenda"

We recently bought a boat and affectionately named her the "No Agenda." She's a dream come true for Lindon. Since getting out of the Coast Guard over twenty years ago, he's dreamed of the day when owning his own boat would become a reality. We both love the water, have lots of time to enjoy boating activities in sunny AZ, and were in the right financial position to make it happen.

As you might imagine, the desire to move forward with this purchase was tugging at us in big way. Long before getting serious about the purchase, though, we talked about how this would affect our daily life, our future plans, our budget, and our family. We were keenly aware that this boat, which had the potential to bring us so much joy and pleasure, could also become the source of much grief and clutter. It was far more than just a financial decision. We can honestly say that even though we both wanted the boat and it was a great deal, we would've passed on it had we felt it would've compromised anything of importance or priority to us.

We seriously considered the purchase for eight months, and by the time we made the final decision, we both felt extremely comfortable and confident with our decision. Yeah, yeah, yeah, we know all the jokes. "The best two days of a boat owner's life are the day he buys it and the day he sells it." "Did you know BOAT stands for Bust Out Another Thousand?" There are many more jabs aimed at boat owners, but talk to any true boat lover and they'll just laugh them off. So far, we're laughing too.

We purchased the boat used; it's eight years old but in spectacular condition and had just over forty hours of use when we got it. Financially, the purchase wouldn't present any challenge at all and we had room in our monthly budget for necessities such as insurance, gas, park entrance fees, repairs, etc. We both have great weekday schedules for work, so our weekends are often free and we knew there would be lots of time to enjoy our boat. Lindon is a bit of a maintenance fanatic and thoroughly enjoys that aspect of owning anything, so even the upkeep required wasn't going to be an issue. And our kids? Well, suffice it to say they were thrilled! Trent's wife, Nicole, told us that the morning after we bought the boat, Trent rolled over in bed, looked lovingly at his wife of six months and said, "I sure have a beautiful wife...AND my family owns a boat!" Boy did we laugh! So far it all sounds pretty good, right? Well, it is, but we'd be remiss if we didn't also share some of the other conversations we had.

I [*Lindon*] enjoy being on the water so much that I could easily go out every weekend and stay all weekend long if my schedule permitted it, but it doesn't. I currently have a commitment to help with the audio for church services on Sunday mornings and am required to be there from 7:30 a.m. until noon every Sunday. Could I see the boat distracting me and encouraging me to slack on my commitment? Absolutely!

And I [*Sherry*] still deal with feelings of guilt when I am "spoiled" with luxury items or blessings that are too wonderful to wrap my head around. Mixed in with my excitement, there was a certain amount of anxiety and apprehension. Did we deserve the boat? Would people think we were being irresponsible making such a purchase in light of the current economy? Would they think less of us? I really struggled with feelings of guilt about having something so nice.

Both of us were concerned that the boat might hinder the time we had for writing and significantly slow down the progress of our book. We were in a pretty good groove and hesitant to do anything that might disrupt that. Honestly, there wasn't much we didn't stop to consider, but in retrospect, that's a good thing. We've got our heads on straight, are aware of the potential pitfalls, and are committed to making sure we keep our eyes on Jesus.

By now you are probably thinking that we are the most neurotic worry warts around, and if our book is encouraging you to operate like us, you're going to high tail it in the opposite direction. It may seem like a lot of time and work leading up to the final decision, but recognize the payoff. When we finally made the decision, we had a peace about it for all the right reasons. We could wholly enjoy the purchase, the process, and the boat. No regrets, no financial stress, no guilt, and no clutter. And guess what? Part of this book even got written while we were on the No Agenda, tucked away in a quiet cove on a desert lake. Perfection!

It's so much easier to take extra time and make good decisions on the front side, than to deal with the clutter and fallout of avoidable mistakes and distractions on the back. In this case, a good thing really was just that—good. Actually, great! We got this one right.

Not so Fast...

Of course it wasn't, and still isn't always, that way. We've each made some decisions we regretted, choices that weren't thought through carefully and brought clutter to our lives while distracting us from our walk and our purpose. We've definitely learned the hard way.

Years ago I [*Lindon*] purchased a new home. I thought I had considered everything—finances, family, neighborhood, lifestyle, wants vs. needs, etc. I had lived in my old home for twelve years and paid my dues. It was a nice, smaller home in a modest neighborhood and served its purpose well, but I was financially solid, the kids were a bit older, and it just seemed time for a fresh start in the kind of place I thought my family deserved. It was a beautiful spec home in a gorgeous new community and what a deal it was!

I paid cash for just about everything I purchased to make the home "ours." I was in my glory working on a respectable landscaping project, complete with putting green, horseshoe pit, lazy river, waterfall, and fire pit. I had visions of this house being the family stop for years to come, the social hot spot where all would gather. It was a grand plan and I pretended I had it all figured out, but deep down inside, I knew differently. With boxes not yet unpacked, I stood out in front of this beautiful home while talking on the phone to my sister. I was telling her how for reasons I didn't understand at the time, I had a feeling I wouldn't be in this house very long. I didn't realize then how incredibly short my stay would be.

Buying that house, I thought I had it all, that I had finally made it. I was living the American dream, right? I had a well-paying job, a house that radiated just a little bit of status, two great kids, and my marriage, well, you can't have everything... It was broken beyond repair, but I wasn't a quitter. Christians don't divorce and I was raised a Christian, counseled by Christians, and felt a responsibility to live up to the expectation of those Christians. What I masked at the time was my decision to settle. I was distracted by the acquisition, in denial about my marriage, and lulled into complacency. It all backfired big time.

I had never wanted to stay in Arizona, but my ex-spouse insisted. I caved and focused on what I thought was the right thing to do, disregarding my true heart and feelings. What I fooled myself into believing was good, ultimately brought more damaging distractions and disruptions to my life than I could've ever imagined. There was so much suffering and pain to come.

The truth was my marriage was in shambles and had been for years. Perhaps the house was my misguided attempt to keep things together? I just wanted everything to be okay, and figured a new beginning might make that become a reality. Nothing could have been further from the truth. Unfortunately, the only one who benefited from the purchase of this gorgeous home was the next owner who got the house for a fraction of what I paid. Within three months of signing the papers and moving in, I was separated, I'd lost my job, and my kids and I were living in an almost empty home that I could no longer afford. The house was so far on the outskirts of town that I couldn't even afford the gas it took to get to the church I'd been attending. The clutter in my life and in my heart was overwhelming. Had I prayerfully and truthfully considered all that I should have, I would have never made the decision to purchase that home and continue the lie I was living.

Miraculously, I never lost sight of God. I knew that he always had his hand on me, and when I didn't make the decisions I should have, God intervened on my behalf. I'm forever grateful for this, but

I wasted a lot of time, energy, and emotion along the way. My head was too cluttered and my life full of too many distractions to apply my full potential for God. He loved me and I knew this, but for me to love and serve him in the way he deserved, I needed to declutter, get my life squared away, and make every moment count with God in the center. It was a slow and steady climb, but I did it. I'm living proof that from the depths of despair, from a horrifically cluttered mess, from both seemingly good distractions and clearly bad ones, you can sift through it all, make better decisions, and become whole again so that God can get your firsts, the best you have to offer. Be on guard and don't let distractions hinder or ruin your "GO Time"!

Ironically, after I finally got to the place where I was free from the past and able to nurture my relationship with God, I've been able to live and experience the most joyful time in my life. And guess what? I still live in sunny Arizona and love it. That's probably the biggest shocker for me. I must admit that given the chance, I wouldn't pass on an ocean side condo, but truly, I'm happy here.

Letting Go and Letting God

It's absolutely mind-blowing what will happen when you declutter and intentionally live for God. Remember that even though you've made decisions to live for God, the timing of what will happen and when is all his! It's tough stuff to be patient and wait for God to act but sometimes that is the intentional part of your living. Letting go and letting God! Let him do his work in and through you. Life is not like a game of monopoly. It's not about the acquisition, having status, or being in control. Contrary to what you may feel or believe, it's not always about getting what you want. The one with the most toys isn't guaranteed to win and isn't necessarily the happiest. It's about your relationship with God. Honor and serve God with a truly contrite and humble spirit, and joy, deep joy, and contentment will enter your life.

Replace the Space with God

Be an empty vessel before Christ. Empty yourself so you can be filled wholly by God. But make certain it's God who is doing the filling. Luke 11:24-26 warns us what can happen when we are (even temporarily) emptied of evil but fail to allow God to fill that emptiness: "When an evil spirit comes out of a man, it goes through arid places seeking rest and does not find it. Then it says, 'I will return to the house I left.' When it arrives, it finds the house swept clean and put in order. Then it goes and takes seven other spirits more wicked than itself, and they go in and live there. And the final condition of that man is worse than the first."

Guarding ourselves from spiritual laziness, we must intentionally choose to be filled with the power of the Holy Spirit. We may even need a practical daily reminder to invite God into our lives and to open ourselves up to all that is good and pleasing to him. Sherry's friend, Stacy, uses such a reminder. Many mornings she turns her coffee mug upside down in a motion indicative of emptying the cup. Then, when she turns it right side up, she prays before pouring coffee into the mug that the Lord would fill her up to overflowing with all that he is and all that he wants her to be. She often includes a friend or two in the request, and Sherry has been the grateful recipient of some of those prayers.

Free to Give God Your All!

In the beginning of this chapter, we joked about game playing with God, but making sure your life is decluttered enough to give God the time and space he deserves is no laughing matter. When you get right down to it, all we have and all we are is from God. Everything from start to finish. The whole kit and caboodle. All the hope we have is because of him and what he's promised us. Our salvation and eternal existence is available because of what he's done on our behalf. The magnitude of what he has and will provide for us is far-reaching and mind-boggling. If you believe this to be true, how could you settle for giving God anything less than your absolute best with a front and center spot in your life? Would you expect God to settle for anything but that? You shouldn't and he won't.

So what's your call on this one? What's it going to be? Your next play should be, "Ready or not, HERE I COME!" Have no fear. God is not only ready for you, but willing and able to accept all the love, devotion, and service you have to offer. He will never abandon you, let you down, or hurt you. He will always protect, comfort, and care for you. The game of life isn't always easy, and there are no guarantees except for the promises in your relationship with Christ.

Declutter your life, and make room for the most important person of all. GO get God! We're praying for you!

Bibliography

"stress." Merriam-Webster. 2012. http://merriam-webster.com (12 January 2012).

"What are the Common Symptoms of Stress" Posted 2012. Symptoms of Stress.com.
www.symptoms-of-stress.com. (Accessed April 12, 2012)

"American Heart Association" Posted 2012.
www.heart.org. (Accessed April 12, 2012)

COMING SOON

Look for the *Declutter Now! Workbook*, perfect for individuals, small groups, and bible studies. Check our website for updates and information: www.actionplanministries.com

For more information about
Lindon & Sherry Gareis
&
Declutter Now!
please visit:

actionplanministries.com
declutternow@actionplanministries.com
@actionplanmin
www.facebook.com/declutternow

. . . .

For more information about
AMBASSADOR INTERNATIONAL
please visit:

www.ambassador-international.com
@AmbassadorIntl
www.facebook.com/AmbassadorIntl